Madeleine
McCann

TEN YEARS ON

Danny Collins

JOHN BLAKE

Published by John Blake Publishing Limited,
3 Bramber Court, 2 Bramber Road,
London W14 9PB, England

www.johnblakebooks.com

www.facebook.com/johnblakebooks 🔲
twitter.com/jblakebooks 🔲

First published in paperback in 2008 as *Vanished*
This edition published in 2017

ISBN: 978-1-78606-272-7

British Library Cataloguing-in-Publication Data:
A catalogue record for this book is available from the British Library.

Design by www.envydesign.co.uk

Printed in Great Britain by CPI Group (UK) Ltd

1 3 5 7 9 10 8 6 4 2

© Text copyright Danny Collins 2008, 2017

The right of Danny Collins to be identified as the author of this work
has been asserted by him in accordance with the Copyright,
Designs and Patents Act 1988.

Papers us⋯ ⋯lucts made
from w⋯ ⋯rocesses
conf⋯ ⋯rigin.

Every a⋯ ⋯holders,
but so⋯ ⋯opriate

J⋯ ⋯g.

For Madeleine
and Jenny Klein, again.

Contents

Acknowledgements

Nine years have passed since this book, or the major part of it, was published. Nine long years during which I have written other books and looked at other cases in my profession as an investigative journalist. Many people have read the story herein and some have said, 'How did you know the truth?' I didn't. I put forward a valid theory based on the evidence available. Some didn't like it; they had their own theories. I acknowledge that.

My publisher has asked me to add some chapters on what has happened during the ten years since the case opened in 2007 and I have complied because I feel the story of Madeleine McCann is important. The case has brought about changes to how police investigate a disappearance. Pauline's Law was introduced in the United States. Any changes to laws are welcome.

I have received correspondence from the parents and relatives of missing persons all over the world. These are the people I would like to acknowledge, along with my book editor, Sarah Fortune, who has nursed me and the book through to the second publication. Others I must thank include the Romanies of Aranjuez who helped me with their theories and Clarence Mitchell, the faithful spokesman of the McCanns.

'Leaving No
Stone Unturned'

The true crime genre of writing must, by its very nature, take as its research material the heartbreak and misery that always relates to a crime, whether the source is the unfortunate victim or the relatives of those who have been snatched from life. As such, we writers may be seen to profit from those miseries, although, in keeping with my fellow scribes, I know that the unravelling of the story and the satisfaction of having achieved a completed and accurate account of the history often overcomes the desire for pecuniary gain. Not always, but often.

In the case of Madeleine McCann, the ultimate reward would be to see this engaging little child reunited with her parents and siblings before yet another anniversary of her disappearance passes. If you would like to help

Madeleine's Fund: 'Leaving No Stone Unturned' in its work or make a donation online, you'll find details at www.findmadeleine.com. The full objectives of the Fund are:

1. To secure the safe return to her family of Madeleine McCann, who was abducted in Praia da Luz, Portugal, on Thursday, 3 May 2007.

2. To procure that Madeleine's abduction is thoroughly investigated and that her abductors, as well as those who played (or play) any part in assisting them are identified and brought to justice.

3. To provide support, including financial assistance, to Madeleine's family.

If the above objects are fulfilled then the objects of the Fund shall be to pursue such purposes in similar cases arising in the United Kingdom, Portugal or elsewhere.

Postal donations can be made with cheques payable to 'Madeleine's Fund: Leaving No Stone Unturned' and sent to: Madeleine's Fund: Leaving No Stone Unturned Limited, PO Box 53133, London E18 2YR or to NatWest, PO Box 113, Cavell House, 2A Charing Cross Road, London WC2H ONN. Sort Code: 60-40-05, Account Number: 32130058
Internet banking donations from abroad to either:
IBAN: GB63 NWBK 6040 0532 1300 58
IBAN: GB63NWBK 6040 0532 1300 58

MADELEINE'S FUND

Sort Code: 60-40-05
Account Number: 32130058
Iban bic: NWBKGB2L
All donations will be processed free of charge and your
generosity is greatly appreciated.

Danny Collins

Preface

This book tells of what happened in the resort of Praia da Luz in Portugal's Algarve region on the evening of 3 May 2007. A British female child had disappeared from the apartment in which she had been holidaying with her parents and siblings, twins Sean and Amelie. This bubbly child, full of fun and giggles, as all three-year-olds are, vanished into thin air and left behind a mystery that has dumbfounded police and the public ever since. It is the story of what happened on that night a decade ago and what has occurred since. It is a faithful recounting of the facts surrounding the child's disappearance, and of the accusations and finger-pointing that followed. It also tells of the investigation by Portuguese police and of the conclusions reached, and closes with the work of Operation Grange, the Scotland Yard inquiry launched by the Metropolitan Police in 2011.

Preface

CHAPTER 1

Still Waters

Ten years have passed since three-year-old Madeleine McCann disappeared from her holiday apartment as her parents sat with friends nearby. Recently, I returned to the resort in which this took place.

Almost ten years ago, I had arrived in Praia da Luz after a 940-kilometre drive along the A-92 at the behest of my publisher who wanted the story of Madeleine's disappearance recorded in time for the first anniversary. I had been working on the text of a book about an English married couple who had gone missing on the Costa Blanca (*Nightmare in the Sun,* John Blake Publishing, 2007). The journey took nearly ten hours.

Praia da Luz, which means 'Beach of Light', is a small, former fishing village and now thriving holiday resort, population 3,500, which lies six kilometres from Lagos in the Algarve of Portugal. Like most settlements it changed its livelihood to a holiday resort with the advent of tourism to south-coastal Iberia in the 1970s. It was the holiday venue chosen by the McCann and their group of professional doctors, a consultant friend and their partners and children for a ten-day holiday in the last week of April and the first week of May 2007.

The young British girl's disappearance and the subsequent inquiry would cause a huge public and press furore, surpassing anything I'd seen in nearly twenty years of journalism. Journalists gyrate around tragedy. We don't live off tragedy any more than radio or television newscasters, but the reader always assumes that we do.

The case of Madeleine McCann is a prime example of plot and counterplot, and of confusion laid by many of the players, each one of whom has resorted to a play on public emotions to win their point. But behind all of this lies the fate of a small child who was miserably failed by those who should have cared for her. Amidst all the talk of guilt and responsibility, of sexual predators who roam the shadows of a popular tourist resort, and of politicians and policemen who fear the smear that could be cast on their country's tourism by such a possibility, the hunt for Madeleine McCann struggles for priority.

And so, as the tenth anniversary of Madeleine's disappearance approached, I went back to the village. I found it structurally unchanged. The scene of the unsolved mystery, the Ocean Club holiday complex still stands, as does the tapa bar where her parents sat, taking part in a quiz night, unaware that their daughter would be gone when they returned to their holiday rental apartment at 5A, Waterside Garden.

I wandered around, noting the areas that figured in the inquiry, like the Rua da Escola Primária, where the Smith family stated to police that they saw a man resembling Gerry McCann carrying a child of Madeleine's description at 10pm as they walked to their holiday apartment from Kelly's Bar on the night she went missing.

I spoke to some locals in one of the bars. They all remembered the hordes of press that descended on the resort in the early summer of that year. But, apart from that, nothing much had changed in Praia da Luz since 2007. You can still eat the grilled, salty sardines in the Paraiso, the beach restaurant located on the pretty south-facing beach where Madeleine McCann played with her twin siblings, Sean and Amelie, on the morning of 3 May 2007, the day she was to disappear and pose the biggest mystery of the decade. The world asked, and is asking still, 'Where is Madeleine? Is she alive?'

Questions like that are still asked in the police station at Portimão, where DCI Gonçalo Amaral once held sway and oversaw the search for the missing three-year-old. It is the same police station that grief-stricken Kate and Gerry McCann, the parents of the missing child, attended on 7 September 2007. They left the marble portal branded *arguidos* – suspects in a disappearance that weighed heavily upon them, evident in the strained features of Kate who clutched a small, forlorn doll, the pink Cuddle Cat, all that remained on the rumpled coverlet of her daughter's bed – a tragic reminder of her presence in the room from which she had disappeared as her siblings slept in a cot nearby.

The McCanns were to receive many harsh public comments because they and the parents in their group had left children unsupervised in apartments while they themselves caroused in a bar. 'Caroused' might seem a strong word for sipping wine and taking part in an organised quiz night, but the criticism became even stronger when it was revealed by the McCanns that they had left a rear patio sliding door unlatched for convenience in checking on the sleeping children. Was the delay in telling the police of the open patio door caused by a fear of prosecution for abandonment or negligence in the care of minors?

Theories about the disappearance of the child abounded, as they do today, but Praia da Luz has weathered the crisis and is the same as in May 2007. If anything has changed it is the gate opening onto the small garden of 5A. The gate is now higher, hiding the once visible steps that led down into the garden, just visible from the bar where Kate and Gerry sat with their companions wining and dining on the fateful late evening of 3 May 2007.

CHAPTER 2

Into Darkness

The eastern Atlantic breeze blew a sultry column of warm air northwards across the 800 metres separating Ocean Club's Waterside Garden complex in Praia da Luz from the curving and broad sandy beach, now deserted as evening fell over the popular resort. At the poolside tapas bar situated between Rua Primero do Maio and Rua Dr Francisco Gentil Martins, a large round table held nine revellers, medical professionals and their partners plus Dianne Webster, mother of Dr Payne's wife Fiona, who were now enjoying an after-dinner quiz night organised by the Ocean Club's aerobics teacher Najova Chekaya.

Waiter José Baptista thought it unusual that the loquacious British group should linger so long every night after dinner at the table they claimed as their own, talking and drinking wine until after 10pm, a time when the local Portuguese or the

Spanish holidaymakers from across the border at Vila Real de San Antonio – where the Guadiana River separates the Iberian neighbours – would be expecting to dine themselves.

But tonight finding vacant tables would be no great problem as only a few were taken up by the group's fellow quiz competitors. This was 3 May and the normally busy resort was still in the low season that wouldn't end until the advent of the official early summer on 25 May. Besides, the group paid well for their occupation of the best poolside table, consuming an average of eight to ten bottles of wine with and after their meals each night.

José noticed one of the men from the group of what he gleaned from the conversation at the table to be doctors raise a finger and indicate an empty wine bottle. He smiled in reply and nodded, crossing over to the wine rack against a wall of the adjoining restaurant to fulfil the order.

That evening the arrivals of the British party at the bar had been erratic. The handsome Scottish consultant Gerry McCann and his slim blonde doctor wife Kate had been first to arrive at around 8.30pm, Dr Oldfield and his wife Rachael followed fifteen minutes later, with a worried Jane Tanner, partner of Dr Russell O'Brien, arriving later with her husband before leaving almost immediately to check on her sick daughter once again.

Gerry McCann went back to check on the children within half an hour of his arrival and, soon after Jane Tanner's return from checking her own sick child, it was the turn of Matthew Oldfield to rise and look at his wristwatch. He said something to the Scottish couple and a woman whom

José assumed was his wife before leaving the table to walk towards the Ocean Club apartments at the head of Rua Dr Francisco Gentil Martins to fulfil his shared obligation of checking the group's children.

Of the group, who had holidayed together in Greece the previous year and found their 'child-watch' system to work admirably with no need of in-house babysitters, only Dr David Payne and his attractive doctor wife Fiona weren't called on to take part in the routine, having invested in a radio baby monitor that worked well at the 100 metres line-of-sight distance to their own apartment in the block. Before the night ended, there were others in the group who would wish they had resorted to such labour-saving technology...

José Baptista shook his head and clicked his tongue in disapproval as Dr Oldfield left the group while checking his own timepiece. It was 9.38pm. He often saw this man and his dark-haired wife during the day sitting near the pool with their two young daughters in company with the Scottish couple and their own three children: Madeleine, a fair-haired, pretty and engaging little girl of three or four years of age, and two equally blond, ever-active younger twins, Sean and Amelie. But, with the exception of the day of the families' joint arrival, the children never accompanied their parents in the evening as was usual with Portuguese families.

It seemed to José that the children were always left alone at night. He had overheard Club staff remark that the late diners never took advantage of the crèche or the on-site offer of babysitters. Instead, they appeared to share a self-imposed monitoring system in which one of the men would leave the table at approximately half-hour intervals that got more erratic as the evening progressed to check on the children. Meanwhile, the little ones were left alone in the empty apartments for up to three hours. Who were these foreigners who would do such a thing?

José Baptista thought of his own large family and the love lavished on his nephews and nieces by his sisters and brothers and their partners. Would a Portuguese child ever be left alone without a friendly ear to hear a cry at night? Sweet Jésu, never! He shook his head in bewilderment and carried on uncorking the wine.

The doctor with the difficult English accent, the one the group called Gerry, had taken his turn to visit the apartments earlier: 9.05pm. If the group stayed drinking and talking to past 10pm as was usual, José supposed Dr Gerry would follow the nightly ritual and his turn would come around again thirty minutes after Dr Oldfield returned.

The rear of apartment blocks 4 and 5 of the Ocean Club's Waterside Garden was outside the complex proper on the other side of the perimeter wall of the pool and restaurant area. To reach them there were two alternate routes: the first was across a grassy area surrounding a small water feature to the left of the large kidney-shaped pool. This led through a large metal gate that gave access to a narrow cobbled walkway passing along the rear of the apartments. The second, more direct route passed to the right of the pool through the Ocean Club security gate at the side of the reception building. From there, the walker would turn left up the hill of Dr Francisco Gentil Martins, following the perimeter wall until it turned sharply to the left at a right angle to form the northern wall of the perimeter, bordering the walkway that ran west to east at the rear of the apartments. Apartment 5A, the McCann's rented accommodation where Madeleine, Sean and Amelie slept, stood on the corner of Block 5, where the walkway abutted the street.

The next-door apartment, 5B, was occupied by Russell O'Brien, who worked as a consultant in Acute Medicine at the Royal Devon and Exeter Hospital, and his partner Jane Tanner and their two children. Further down the walkway were the apartments of his colleagues Drs David and Fiona Payne, and then the apartment where Dr Oldfield's own offspring now lay sleeping.

Much debate has surrounded the distance that the tapas bar lies from the McCanns' corner apartment. The circuitous route to the left of the pool was longer at 180 metres but more convenient for checking the rear of the apartments where the children of both families slept – a distance later to be ignored by journalists who guesstimated the direct line-of-sight route from the tapas bar to be anything between 40 and 80 metres, not taking into account that anyone pursuing that route would eventually be faced with a climb over a 1.4-metre wall. The shorter route, through the reception security gate and up the hill, was the one favoured by the McCanns. These areas and access to the private pool were regularly patrolled by Ocean Club security guards.

Dr Matthew Oldfield, who worked at Kingston Hospital in that part of Surrey now swallowed up into south-west London, was holidaying with his wife, City headhunter and former lawyer Rachael Oldfield, and their children. He approached the rear-facing apartments shrouded from the view of the poolside revellers by a thick hedge of exotic pink and white oleander blossoms backed by low bushes and trees running along the pool's northern perimeter, effectively cutting off the sight of anyone entering or leaving the apartments by the elevated rear patios.

Amid all the confusion that would later surround the distance from the rear of apartment 5A to the tapas bar, the Ocean Club plan of the Waterside Garden complex shows it to be approximately 120 metres. I spoke with an employee of the Club in Praia da Luz and asked if she would be so kind as to check out the security gate approach by walking the route. She timed the walk at two minutes and 30 seconds.

On the night of 3 May, Dr Oldfield entered the gate off the walkway into the small rear garden and followed the steps up to his own patio. He then stepped inside his family holiday apartment, where he checked his children were sleeping soundly and then returned to the lights of the tapas bar by way of the reception security gate after he'd checked that the children slept soundly in the McCanns' apartment.

According to his statement, given on 4 May 2007 to Portuguese police, Matthew Oldfield said he took his turn at checking the children at 9.45pm. He entered the rear garden of apartment 5A and climbed the steps to the rear patio of the apartment. There, he put his ear to the left-hand sliding glass panel and frame to listen for any sound within the apartment. He heard nothing and assumed the children inside were sleeping on, undisturbed. Following this, he then walked back to the bar and raised his thumb towards his friends, Gerry and Kate McCann, before reclaiming his chair and a freshly filled glass.

At the tapas bar, the conversation and laughter continued and Kate McCann glanced at her watch, noting the hour was after 10pm. Her husband Gerry was in the middle of a story involving an incident at the Glenfield Hospital at Leicester where he was employed as a consultant cardiologist. Not wanting to break into his monologue or disturb the company, Kate rose from the table and made her way around the pool and through the security gate to walk up the hill to the apartments. José Baptista was surprised by her departure: he had never known her to check on the children before.

On reaching the apartment, mounting the steps and sliding open the unlocked patio door, Kate was struck by a sense of stillness. She made her way across the dining area to the front bedroom on the left, where she had settled Madeleine and the twins before leaving for the restaurant with Gerry. Now the twins slept on in their cots but Madeleine's bed was empty.

Kate moved quickly through the rooms of the small rented apartment calling her daughter's name. The twins stirred and began to whimper. She frantically checked the bathroom, and her own and Gerry's bedroom, pulling up the bedclothes and looking under the bed frame before rooting through wardrobes. Panic overtook her. Her hysterical shouts that someone – 'they' was the word Charlotte Pennington would recall – had taken her daughter and her repeated cries of Madeleine's name now rising to hysteria brought Pennington, an on-duty childminder on watch in a nearby apartment.

Confusion continued to reign as the alerted diners rapidly sobered up and found themselves, along with staff and residents, wandering the nearby streets of the resort calling out the lost child's name. For many, their first thought, despite Kate McCann's alleged dramatic outburst to the childminder, was that little Madeleine must have woken up and gone out into the night looking for her parents. The streets stood dimly muted in the soft amber streetlights and the beach reflected only the light of the moon and the murmuring of the Atlantic surf. Madeleine McCann was gone.

CHAPTER 3

First Report

I n those first stunned moments when the realisation
dawned that Madeleine had disappeared from apartment 5A, there was a frenzied search of the small gardens,
hardly more than paved enclosures, at the rear of blocks 4
and 5. It is likely someone would have walked further up
the hill of Dr Francisco Gentil Martins and turned left and
left again into the car-parking area fronting the apartment
blocks. The streets around the Waterside Garden complex in
Praia da Luz are well lit at night but every urban development
has its shadows.

There seemed no doubt that Madeleine had walked out
of the apartment through the unlocked rear patio doors. No
one, except it seemed the child's parents, could contemplate
the horror of abduction. Madeleine was just a little girl. Who
would take her and why? However, an even grimmer truth

was descending on the McCanns and their friends. Six of the group – the McCanns, the Oldfields, Russell O'Brien and his partner Jane Tanner – had left their children alone in unlocked apartments for up to three hours every one of the five evenings since their arrival at the resort. Now one of the children was missing. How would the Portuguese police, let alone the uncles, aunts and grandparents of their charges, view this? Was it even possible that each and every one of them would end up in a Portuguese jail for child endangerment? No one knew how the law stood on that particular theme in Portugal and it seemed not the most propitious time to put it to the test. Madeleine was gone and the police had to be informed and statements taken. However, it is unclear whether police attending were aware that the patio doors of apartment 5A had been left unlocked. Although it was obvious that Madeleine could not have walked out of a locked apartment, the Guarda Nacional Republicana (GNR) officers first on the scene may have assumed that the simple up-down interior latch of the patio door would have proved no insurmountable difficulty for a determined and intelligent three-year-old. Alternatively, it appeared that the front door to the apartment, which opened on to a parking lot at the front of the building, was ajar. This, as in the case of the open window, may have occurred before the police arrived during the first frantic search for the missing child. What is apparent is that the officers of the GNR were certain Madeleine had somehow left the apartment and would be found wandering in the nearby streets. However, Judicial Police who would arrive on the scene later were equally unaware that the patio door had been left unlocked and, discarding the possibility that the child could have opened it herself, were left with the darker suspicions of their calling. The front-door exit was only later considered unlikely when a rumour was spread by the press that the front doors of the apartments required the use of a key turned on the inside to open them, but this only proved to be an illustration of how quickly reporting of the case turned to creative copy due to the lack of information coming out of Portimão. The fictional note of that report was crushed when the Praia da Luz mayor, Manuel Domingues Borba, pointed out that such a means of exit would never have got past his council's building and fire regulations. Thus, back to a front-door exit, but the method of entry was still in doubt.

The McCanns were an intelligent couple. He was a consultant cardiologist and she worked as a general medical practitioner; both were university graduates but they knew nothing about the sinister art of housebreaking. In their panic and desire to avoid condemnation for their ill-considered negligence, they overlooked the simplest of truths that would later be seized on by the Portuguese investigators and see them considered prime suspects in their daughter's disappearance: the metal shutters installed on the windows of apartment blocks 4 and 5 of the Montes da Luz urbanisation housing apartment 5A were impossible to lever upwards more than one or two centimetres. Nor did the shutters or the sills on which they rested in the closed position show any marks of an attempt at forced entry. The Judicial Police called to the scene were immediately suspicious: how could someone spirit a child away through locked doors?

15

Even more suspicious and confusing were the statements of the McCanns' companions, obviously close friends of the missing child's parents. In the week following Madeleine's disappearance when the public finally learned the truth about the patio doors, the statements of some of the friends changed dramatically. Matthew Oldfield told police that he merely listened at the rear of the apartment for any sound from the McCann children, but now he reorganised his statement and claimed he had walked into the apartment through the unlocked patio doors and listened at the half-open bedroom door. But he too was unaware the investigators hadn't bought the story of a jemmied shutter.

This time he assured police that he had in fact entered the apartment and looked into the bedroom by the light of the open shutter. He admitted to seeing the twins in their cots but, inexplicably, couldn't see Madeleine's bed, although this would have been in full view from the doorway where he stood. It was obvious that his second statement contained certain inconsistencies that would alert the suspicions of the Portuguese Judicial Police, now unconvinced of the possibility of abduction. Such were the suspicions aroused by the witnesses' assertion of a forced shutter that reported sightings supporting the likelihood of abduction were ignored.

Jane Tanner, recounting her earlier trip to check on her own daughter, told disbelieving police that she saw a 'dark-haired man of about thirty-five' carrying a child near the McCanns' apartment but thought nothing of it at the time. Although her report is still taken seriously by UK police, it is possible that the man she saw was British holidaymaker Jeremy Wilkins carrying his eight-month-old son while taking an after-dinner stroll.

Mr Wilkins would also tell investigators that he had spoken to Gerry McCann, with whom he played tennis earlier, when the latter exited 5A at around 9.05pm, although he has no recollection of bumping into Jane Tanner. He told police, 'It was a very narrow path and I think it would have been almost impossible for anyone to walk by without me noticing.'

While his statement doesn't deny the possibility that Jane Tanner may have glimpsed Mr Wilkins as he passed the end of the walkway, this does bring forward the possibility that Madeleine may have exited the apartment by the rear patio door and been picked up in the street by a stranger, whom Jane Tanner glimpsed crossing the end of the walkway to walk south on Dr Francisco Gentil Martins.

While pyjama-clad Madeleine's exit from the gate on to the street and subsequent encounter with a passing sociopath would call for a belief in the most inopportune of coincidences – something in which a good investigator should never believe – a statement taken from Pamela Fenn, occupier of the apartment above the McCanns, demonstrates the child was not beyond going into the street and walkway alone against her parents' wishes.

Pamela Fenn spoke of Madeleine as an often-fractious child, whom she had heard crying for an hour and a quarter on one occasion when she had apparently been left alone in the apartment for an evening with the twins. Local gossip also speaks of an excitable child, who on one occasion escaped from the apartment as bedtime threatened and, giggling with delight at the adventure, hid along the walkway, skipping from garden to garden for thirty minutes before being caught by her parents.

The latter escapade removes any lingering doubt as to whether the engaging three-year-old was adventurous enough to leave the apartment unaccompanied to look for her parents, given the opportunity presented by the unlocked patio door. Assuming the McCanns were aware of Praia da Luz's opportunistic alley-cat community and slid the patio door closed enough to bar them entry to the apartment, the remaining gap would still have been sufficiently wide to allow tiny fingers to enter and pull the door that few centimetres wide enough to allow exit to a determined 35-pound three-year-old.

If indeed the man Jane Tanner, or at least the later witnesses, reported seeing at the rear of the McCanns' apartment was carrying Madeleine, it must be assumed this person, more likely an opportunistic traveller, chanced upon her wandering in the street, since a supposed intruder, having entered the apartment and taken the child, would have exited by the obvious escape route of the front door and hence to a vehicle in which he would have driven north to leave the resort.

There is no recollection of the window being opened or closed by others including the GNR officers who searched the flat, although one might assume that the window would be open at that point, having been opened by someone to check if Madeleine was hiding in the gap between the building and the low wall separating the building from the car-parking area at the front.

Gerry McCann would recall that the shutter was closed when he looked in on his children at 9.05pm, recounting in a phone call that night to his elder sister Trish in the UK: 'I went back to check the children at nine o'clock. They were all sound asleep, windows shut, shutters shut...' But he later told police he noticed the bedroom door was ajar when earlier he and Kate had left it closed. This would prompt him later to say that he believed Madeleine's abductor was already in the room, standing behind the door, when he checked on the children. Should this have been a reality, it would be an agonising thought that would haunt a parent forever, but in all probability he was mistaken. Had the door been opened by Madeleine herself when she went in search of her parents? If so, why didn't Gerry McCann notice his daughter was missing from her bed? It is in these details that the statements of Gerry and Kate McCann and those of their holiday companions would differ sufficiently to place a cloud of suspicion over events that night.

As any investigator of burglary knows, on entering a building the first move of the intruder is to prepare an escape route in the event that he or she has to leave in a hurry. With regard to the McCanns' alleged intruder, this would almost certainly have been the bedroom shutter which Kate was to say she found open an hour later. If this were so, the fact that it was closed when Gerry checked the apartment at 9.05pm makes it unlikely an intruder had entered the building at that time, although in those first hours the couple seemed vague as to whether the window was left open and the shutter closed to ventilate the bedroom when they left the apartment earlier.

Far more likely is the probability that, if abduction occurred from inside the apartment, the intruder entered when Gerry left, with Matthew Oldfield's time-saving listening at the door leaving the abductor undisturbed within the apartment between the visits of Madeleine's parents: a period of almost an hour. But it is far more likely that Madeleine had already left the apartment and met her kidnapper, as fate seemed to have ordained.

Yet again accounts of that fateful night were to differ. According to Ocean Club childminder Charlotte Pennington who was babysitting in a nearby apartment, she was alerted by Kate McCann's screams from the rear balcony of apartment 5A. She told police that, when she arrived at the apartment, Kate clutched at her and sobbed in panic as she tried to answer the childminder's questions. 'They've taken her, they've taken her!' the distraught mother allegedly sobbed. 'Madeleine's gone!'

However, Kate's dinner companions would remember a different scenario. According to those questioned by police on the day following the disappearance, they recalled a distraught Kate running into the tapas bar shouting, 'Madeleine's gone! Madeleine's gone!' This version also matches Kate's own account that she gave to police immediately following her discovery that her daughter was no longer in the apartment, despite the arriving officers' refusal to believe they were dealing with abduction.

However, a third version was to come from a second

waiter at the tapas bar, who claimed he left José Baptista to continue clearing up tables and ran directly towards the sound of the screaming coming from the apartments on the other side of the perimeter wall. He agreed with Charlotte Pennington in that he remembers 'Sra McCann screaming, "They've taken her! They've taken her!"'

Later those conflicting recollections of an understandably distraught mother were seized on by investigators when the McCanns became the focus of enquiries.

The Portuguese police now believed Matthew Oldfield's second statement in which he recalled entering the apartment and listening at the slightly ajar bedroom door, from where he could see the sleeping forms of the twins *by the light of the opened shutter*, was given in support of the McCanns' assertion that the bedroom shutter had been forced open. An indication, if the doctor was to be believed – and he wasn't to be by the Portuguese police – that the intruder was already in the apartment and possibly standing behind the door as Matthew Oldfield looked into the bedroom rather than when Gerry McCann stood at the door half an hour earlier.

Dr Oldfield's second statement bolsters the abductor theory against the possibility of a wandering child meeting up with an opportunistic sociopath in the street – incidentally the probability that Madeleine left the apartment of her own volition was the first and most logical thought of Guarda Nacional Republicana officers arriving at the scene.

But it is only on the open-window theory – which demands utter faith in Dr Oldfield's second statement since no one seems clear whether the window was open or closed when the police first arrived – that the latter theory can be discounted. The most likely possibility is that Dr Oldfield's first statement is the true account of his movements, perhaps later unclear to him in the confusion that was to follow, that he never entered the apartment and the shutter remained closed through the evening only to be opened by the McCanns themselves, or in the resulting confusion by someone seeking signs of an exit route for Madeleine's supposed abductor.

This leads to the likelihood that Madeleine McCann woke up to find herself alone and, demonstrating the determination and sense of adventure that she had shown earlier, wandered out of the apartment into Rua Dr Francisco Gentil Martins in search of her absent parents. From there, she was taken and carried off.

Certain witnesses would later come forward to tell police they had seen a man carrying a child around the time of Madeleine's disappearance. One of them would be an Irish holidaymaker, who would appear much later in the inquiry to tell UK and Portuguese police that he had actually spoken to the man concerning the child's welfare but the man had turned away with his burden and hurried off.

What is clear is that total confusion reigned in and around apartment 5A that night. Just who called the police to report the child missing in that atmosphere of panic has never been satisfactorily resolved. Kate McCann insists the police were informed within ten minutes of her finding her daughter gone, possibly by Charlotte Pennington, the Ocean Club childminder who was first on the scene, although this would normally – if anything could be judged normal that night – have been the responsibility of the resort manager, once roused.

Gerry McCann's version differs in that he believes it was a friend in the group who alerted resort manager John Hill and the police. Neither of these statements matches the timescale of the Portuguese police, which coincides more closely with the account of the waiter who had responded to Kate McCann's screams, who says he himself called the police at 10.40pm, half an hour after the disappearance of the child was announced.

But, according to paramilitary Guarda Nacional Republicana police spokesman Lieutenant Colonel Costa Cabral, the first call was received at GNR HQ at 11.50pm, again nearly two hours after Madeleine was found missing. The police log for 3 May 2007 notes the disappearance occurred 'by 22.40', which coincides more closely with the waiter's statement.

According to the GNR version, police were on the scene by midnight, within ten minutes of the alleged alert and the investigation unit was in full operation by 12.30am. In their confusion, and possibly in the belief that Madeleine left the apartment to look for her parents, the unit failed to recognise apartment 5A and its environs as the scene of a crime. Officers, Ocean Club staff and neighbours were allowed to move freely in and out of the apartment, with police questioning and sympathisers making tea and coffee or offering comfort to the McCanns.

Guilhermino Encarnação, director of the Judicial Police in Faro, who would oversee the initial investigation led by DCI Gonçalo Amaral, said his officers arrived within ten minutes of being alerted and an investigation unit was in operation half an hour later.

But if the bedroom shutters and a window were open when the police arrived no one could recall if this had been done to ventilate the room by a member of the public or whether an intruder deliberately risked the squeal of the plastic rollers to let in light, the better to seek his or her victim rather than risk a light switch or torch beam that might be spotted by a curious passer-by.

The anomaly was highlighted by the fact that a senior detective later at the scene, Judicial Police Deputy Commander and Assistant National Director of the force Paulo Rebelo, would be seen to pass a blanket-wrapped bundle with the approximate dimensions of a three-year-old child through the window that *he himself* opened as if testing a possible exit for the kidnapped child to be passed to an accomplice when the obvious means of exit for an adult carrying a child would have been through the front door to a car or van waiting in the car park.

However, this scenario, which was merely a more complex version of the one involving a wandering Madeleine McCann being picked up and carried off in the street – a much more credible possibility given the truth of the open patio doors – was judged impossible by detectives in the first hours of the investigation. Having caught them out in their assertion that a shutter had been forced, no one in Portimão was going to give the McCanns the benefit of the doubt.

CHAPTER 4

Looking
for Zebras

To further weaken the abduction from inside theory, one might wonder how the intruder entered the apartment unseen. The side steps leading up the unlocked patio door were accessed by a small gate off Dr Francisco Gentil Martins and within 60 metres of the beat of a security guard whose function was to stop unauthorised persons entering the Ocean Club complex by the security gate or via the walkway that passed the rear of the McCanns' apartment. A CCTV camera guarding the pool's walkway entrance was found to be out of order.

Despite some hysterical press reports to the contrary, the shutters of the bedroom window had not been jemmied open from the outside. It therefore follows that the gate on the main street would have been the only entrance to the apartment through the rear garden possibly unobserved by the guard, provided there was sufficient diversion or he had slipped off for a coffee and a cigarette – not an unknown occurrence in laidback Portugal. It was certainly the only route into the apartment worth risking by a determined would-be abductor. But the rear steps to the street would have been too dangerous for a person seeking concealment to exit while carrying a blanket-wrapped child, offering as they did the very real chance of meeting members of the McCann party as they returned from the pool to their apartments; in which case, once inside, the front door that opened on to the car-park area would have seemed the most logical route of retreat. Despite Inspector Rebelo's makeshift reconstruction of the window scenario, the surrounding area was not at once cordoned off with police tape nor was there any immediate attempt to dust the shutter and sill of the window or the front-door lock for fingerprints until many days later. As police spokesman DCI de Sousa would later bemoan, vital evidence that might have supported the theory of abduction was ignored and the entire crime scene compromised from the earliest hour of the investigation.

Most important to experienced investigators, once it was established that the child had not walked into the protective arms of a sympathetic neighbour after being found wandering the street, would have been to notify police on the Spanish border and to monitor all airports and seaports within Portuguese control. What is known of that night is that more than sixty staff and guests at the Ocean Club complex searched the surrounding areas until dawn. As to border and airport alerts, there is serious doubt whether this procedure was implemented during that timescale. One might even be moved to wonder if the non-existence of a forced shutter had so firmly focused the spotlight on the McCanns that the Judicial Police didn't consider a border blockade worth the bother. The answer to that is probably resting among the reams of case notes in Portimão. Portuguese police have yet to supply a definitive timeline of orders and instructions issued that night.

However, what would later especially interest the floundering Portuguese police was why, if one is to believe the childminder and the waiter, did Kate McCann refer to 'they' in her panicked claim that her daughter had been taken? Just who were 'they'? Or were these persons the logical nightmare figures of a protective mother who feared that one day her beautiful daughter would disappear – not an altogether unreasonable concern given the horrors of today's society. It should also be taken into account that language can often cause some misapprehension on the part of native witnesses, interpreters and police interrogators. The undefined 'they' is a common figure of speech in the English language but it would translate as identifiable persons in Portuguese. Whether or not she actually uttered them, those words were to come back to haunt Kate McCann months on into the investigation.

Another question from the police that would later tip the spotlight towards Gerry and Kate McCann as suspects in their daughter's disappearance is how Madeleine, a child described by locals as one who didn't always settle, and the twins Sean and Amelie could sleep so well through the noise and trauma of an abduction. These suspicions again revolve around the supposition that the abduction actually took place. The probability that the twins and Madeleine would have woken up *had an abduction occurred* and was therefore a good indicator that one *hadn't taken place* didn't seem to have entered the investigators' heads.

While no evidence has ever been found that the McCann children were mildly drugged that night – a toxicology test on Sean and Amelie showed they had never been given sedatives of any sort – there can, in any case, be little blame levied at parents who occasionally administer night-time medication to children such as Madeleine, described as 'excessively active' in her mother's spiral-bound diary, provided such administrations are carefully monitored. Although the possibility of the McCanns using commercially produced medication to lull their sometimes overactive children to sleep has been roundly condemned by parents reading the reports, similarly to their leaving the children unmonitored, this has a touch of a suppressed 'there but for the grace of God go I' about it.

While much speculation would later surround the announcement by Portuguese police that samples of blood found not in the apartment, which were later proved to be of masculine gender as described elsewhere, but in the boot of the hired Renault showed 'significant traces of sedatives' in blood alleged to be Madeleine's, shortly afterwards National Director of the Judicial Police Alípio Ribeiro admitted the tests were inconclusive and experts warned of the danger of contamination.

Speaking in an interview with Sir Trevor McDonald on ITN's *Tonight* programme, Professor Allan Jamieson, who has testified about the reliability of DNA in several high-profile cases and is chair of the Standards Committee and Education Group of the Forensic Science Society, stated that he considered it impossible for any expert in the field to tell the concentration of a drug from a dried blood spot. He went on to explain, 'If you have a volume of blood you can calculate the concentration in the blood, but if all you have is a dried blood spot then you wouldn't know the volume of blood that created that; therefore, you would not know the concentration of drug in the blood. And that is important in terms of its toxicological effect.'

Asked whether it was possible to tell if blood had come from a living person or was the result of a post-mortem leak from a corpse, Professor Jamieson continued, 'From a living, breathing individual the issue would be neat blood. When someone dies, the body begins to break down and it is possible that that blood could become mixed with other body fluids. How would you establish that it had become mixed with other body fluids? I don't know how you would do that.' He also insisted it was not possible to detect a one-off dose of sedatives in a hair sample, as this would not have been in the body for a sufficient time for the hair to absorb definable traces.

But with the Portuguese investigators led by DCI Gonçalo Amaral seizing on unformed theories to feed to the media and words of caution from the British police forensic teams unheeded, the case against Gerry and Kate McCann would eventually grow, like Parkinson's law on workloads, to fit the unfettered space fate had prepared for it. It seemed the Portuguese police, having heard hoof beats, were on the lookout for zebras rather than horses. The case files were passed to Judge Pedro Miguel dos Anjos Frias of Portimão's Court of Criminal Instruction. In the meantime, with the investigation stagnated during the first crucial twenty-four hours when an unsolved crime has far more chance of reaching a credible solution, what lay ahead was a mystery that would grow to capture the attention of the world.

CHAPTER 5

Political Chess

In order to understand the politics that have affected the fate of the principal players in the Madeleine McCann saga, it is necessary to appreciate the political fortunes that can be won or lost if Portugal is found guilty of harbouring a paedophile who would snatch a three-year-old foreign child from her bed in one of the country's most affluent tourist regions. Portugal's main capita income originates from the service industry, of which tourism forms the major part of a £2.8 billion turnover. Pressure to come up with a clean slate, especially with a major trial of the Casa Piá paedophile predators due to start in 2008, was enormous. The Casa Pia trial was then to reopen in 2010, after a calamitous start, with the two major protagonists, Jorge Ritto and Carlos Cruz, receiving heavy sentences.

Portugal saw its move to democracy from the authoritarian

rule of President Marcelo Caetano in 1974 when a left-wing military-led coup was christened the Carnation Revolution as young people placed flowers in the muzzles of the soldiers' rifles and invited them to join in freeing the country from Caetano's dictatorial rule. Transition from authoritarian to military rule worried Portugal's allies in the North Atlantic Treaty Organisation (NATO) but the new constitution of 1976 declared the country a democratic republic and Europe and North America breathed a collective sigh of relief.

The country's move from authoritarian rule to provisional military government and on to a parliamentary democracy involved some initial communist and left-wing influence, much to the disquiet of another authoritarian dinosaur, Generalísimo Francisco Franco Bahamonde, in neighbouring Spain. There is no doubt that fear of a communist regime just over the border moved Franco, fast approaching his dotage – he was to die peacefully in Madrid in October 1975 – to move into the shadow of NATO and to open Spain to foreign tourism, thus creating a rivalry between the two countries that exists to this day. The Portuguese Constitution has undergone a number of reforms since, especially in 1989, but these were mainly cosmetic. The original constitution remains the same.

The prospect of a communist takeover in Portugal also prompted considerable concern among the country's NATO allies. The revolution led to the country abruptly abandoning its overseas colonies and to the return of an estimated 600,000 Portuguese citizens from self-imposed exile abroad. The 1976 constitution was revised in 1982, 1989, 1992,

1997, 2001 and 2004, with the 1982 revision, much to the relief of NATO and her allies, placing the military under strict civilian control, trimming the powers of the President and abolishing the Revolutionary Council, a non-elected committee with legislative veto powers.

Much to the delight of the barely emancipated agricultural community, the country joined the European Union in 1986, beginning a path towards greater economic and political integration with its more prosperous European neighbours. Finally, to the relief of Europe, the 1989 revision of the constitution eliminated much of the remaining Marxist rhetoric of the original document, abolished the communist-inspired 'agrarian reform' – always a favourite of a left-wing coup – and laid the groundwork for further privatisation of nationalised firms and the government-owned communications media. The 1992 revision made it compatible with the Maastricht treaty.

The current Portuguese constitution provides for progressive administrative decentralisation and calls for future reorganisation on a regional basis. The Azores and Madeira islands have constitutionally mandated autonomous status. A regional autonomy statute in 1980 established the Government of the Autonomous Region of the Azores; the Government of the Autonomous Region of Madeira operates under a provisional autonomy statute in effect since 1976. Apart from the Azores and Madeira, the country is divided into eighteen districts, each headed by a governor appointed by the Minister of Internal Administration. Macao, a former dependency, reverted to Chinese sovereignty in December

1999, two years after its neighbour Hong Kong. The Algarve – the backcloth to the Madeleine McCann inquiry – is a regional autonomy that coincides with the district of Faro, the city forming its administrative centre. Judicial police involved in the McCann inquiry are deployed from Faro and the investigation is based at Portimão, the most convenient local Judicial Police station to Praia da Luz.

Under the leadership of Antonio Guterres, the Socialist Party came to power in Portugal following the October 1995 parliamentary elections. Later, the Socialists gained a new mandate by winning exactly half the parliamentary seats in the October 1999 election and constituting the XIV Constitutional Government. Socialist Jorge Sampaio had won the February 1992 presidential elections with nearly 54 per cent of the vote. Sampaio's election marked the first time since the 1974 revolution that a single party held prime ministership, the presidency and a plurality of the municipalities. Local elections were held in December 1997.

Prime Minister Guterres continued the privatisation and modernisation policies begun by his predecessor Anibal Cavaco Silva of the Social Democratic Party, an admirer of the policies of former British Prime Minister Margaret Thatcher. He was a vigorous proponent of the effort to include Portugal in the first round of countries to collaborate and put into effect the Euro in 1999. In international relations, Guterres pursued strong ties with the US and greater Portuguese integration with the European Union while continuing to raise Portugal's profile through an activist foreign policy. One of his first decisions as Prime Minister was to send 900 troops to participate in the IFOR peacekeeping mission in Bosnia. Portugal later contributed 320 troops to SFOR, the follow-up Bosnian operation, and also donated aircraft and personnel to NATO's Operation Allied Force in Kosovo.

The XV Constitutional Government, elected in 2002, was led by José Manuel Durão Barroso, leader of the Social Democratic Party in coalition with the People's Party, whose leader Paulo Portas became Minister of Defence. This was also the time when the tightly sealed rumours of sexual abuse of orphans housed at Lisbon's Casa Pia institute escaped from the can where they had been interned since Marcelo Caetano's dictatorship ended in 1974. Many of the outgoing socialist ministers turned out to be involved in the scandal as well as some of the incoming political victors about to occupy positions of power.

After José Manuel Durão Barroso accepted the invitation to be the next European Commission President, a new government had to be formed, at which the opposition parties called for a general election. Instead, long-serving President Jorge Sampaio nominated the new Social Democratic leader Pedro Santana Lopes to form a new government in which Paulo Portas kept his place as Minister of Defence. However, in December 2004, due to several scandals involving the government, including the emerging furore surrounding the Casa Pia revelations, President Sampaio dissolved Parliament and called for early elections. Nevertheless, Santana Lopes resigned after the announcement of the President's decision.

In the ensuing elections of 20 February 2005, the Socialist Party obtained its largest victory ever, achieving an absolute majority for the first time in the party's history. José Sócrates was sworn in by President Jorge Sampaio on 12 March. To the surprise of many observers Sócrates formed a cabinet made up of roughly half the senior members of the Socialist Party and half independents, among them Diogo Freitas de Amaral – no relation to the chubby McCann investigator – who was founder of the People's Party. He was chosen to be Minister of Foreign Affairs but later resigned due to personal issues.

The President, currently Marcelo Rebelo de Sousa, is elected to a five-year term by direct public vote and is also the Commander in Chief of the Armed Forces. Presidential powers include the appointment of the Prime Minister and Council of Ministers, in which the President must be guided by the assembly election results; dismissing the Prime Minister, dissolving the assembly to call early elections, vetoing legislation (which may be overridden by the Assembly) and declaring a state of war or siege.

The Council of State, a presidential advisory body, is composed of six senior civilian officers, any former presidents elected under the 1976 constitution, five members chosen by the Assembly and five selected by the President.

The government is headed by the presidential-appointed Prime Minister, currently António Costa, who names the Council of Ministers. A new government is required to define the broad outline of its policy in a programme and present it to the assembly for a mandatory period of debate. Failure of the Assembly to reject a programme by a majority of deputies confirms the government in office. It was into this political mix of plot, counterplot and ambitions that the ingredients of the McCann inquiry would be added on a weekly basis to produce a dish to suit the developing political palate.

Portugal occupies a fifth of the Iberian Peninsula from its larger neighbour Spain, which borders the country to the north and east. To the west is the wild Atlantic Ocean, whose blistery bite is broken in the south by the spidery point of Punto de Sagres, the westernmost cape in the Gulf of Cádiz, whose easternmost point is formed by the Cape of Trafalgar and neighbouring Gibraltar. The resulting bay of the Costa da Luz – the Coast of Light – is a haven of long sandy beaches and gentle seas that can turn upon ships with fury when storms rise in the south-west, but from April to September the area is a retreat for tourists wishing to escape the chill of northern Europe to a country with a laidback lifestyle and sunshine as well the Euro.

The resorts inhabiting the coastline from east to west are many. Among them are Faro, Albufeira, Lagao, the old slave port of Lagos, a grim reminder of Portugal's involvement in the eighteenth- and nineteenth-century slave trade from Africa, Loulé, Olhau, Portimão, Quartiera, Silves, Tavira and the border town of Vila Real de San Antonio. Occupying Arabs of the eighth to twelfth century AD named this coast *Al-Garb*, which means the west.

The Algarve is hilly but traversed by steep, rich valleys. Its highest point is the inland range of Monchique, an extinct volcanic crop whose lava once flowed south to form the eastern corner of Praia da Luz, the tiny Beach of Light to the west of Portimão. This entire region covers an area of approximately 5,400 square metres with 410,000 registered inhabitants but, like the neighbouring Costas of Spain, the actual number is probably as much as doubled by the eternal tourist, that eccentric species of northern expatriate who prefers not to enter the system. At the height of the summer season, the influx of tourists can reach more than one million.

Of the resorts dotted along the coast, Praia da Luz, a few scant kilometres from Lagos, is a holiday destination that draws many Portuguese as well as British, French and German families. Their main destination is the Ocean Club complex. Dating from the 1980s, the Ocean Club is split into four different areas within the village and made up of holiday apartments and self-catering villas. The result of the division of holiday accommodation around the locality is to give an atmosphere of being part of the community of a small fishing village, although the fantasy is marred by the fact that most of the estimated 10,000 permanent residents of Praia da Luz are British, Dutch and German expatriates.

A flaw in this layout is the security of the complex, which calls for private security guards to prevent non-guests entering Ocean Club facilities such as swimming pools and lounging areas. Many of the apartments and villas are privately owned and, in 2007, were rented out to the Mark Warner holiday company for the season. Such was 5A, located just outside the perimeter of the Waterside Garden restaurant and pool complex. A ground-floor two-bedroom apartment separated from the pool area by a chest-high whitewashed wall and thick bushes, ten days' half board for a family of two adults (all children under five at the Ocean Club go free) would then cost in the region of £1,600. For this, parents also enjoyed the benefit of free evening childcare in a crèche if they dined at one of the Club's four restaurants and, for a small charge, the Club also provided an individual babysitting service that could be booked at the nearby reception office.

Although the services were provided free or at little cost, the McCanns and their holiday companions, all of whom had young children, chose to take turns in checking on the children throughout the evening with the exception of David Payne and his wife, who were using an intermediate-range radio baby monitor. For the others, it appeared that checking the children in their own way had worked well on a visit to Greece in the previous year and no one saw any reason to change it except perhaps the more security-conscious Paynes.

The distance from the tapas bar at the Waterside Garden complex and apartment 5A set outside the complex perimeter wall on the corner of two streets is 120 metres. The lower floor of the apartment block, the only one let out to Warner with others in the five-storey block occupied by their owners, was not visible from the restaurant. It was for this reason that the holiday complex provided a crèche and babysitter service popular with guests, but not taken up on this occasion by the McCann party.

A seemingly thoughtless and naive action that would bring widespread acrimony on the group was seen as even more irresponsible in the eyes of the public, who would soon learn of Madeleine McCann's apparent abduction. In their haste to carry out the checks with little inconvenience to themselves, the holidaying parents had left the rear patio doors of the apartments ajar.

CHAPTER 6

The Investigation

Heading up the investigation into the supposed abduction of Madeleine McCann from apartment 5A that night was Chief Inspector of Judicial Police Gonçalo Amaral. The Judicial Police, who have control over cases of a criminal nature in Portugal, differ from the Guarda Nacional Republicana, which has a paramilitary role in keeping the peace outside the mandate of the towns and cities in a role akin to that of the Guardia Civil in Spain.

The first police officer on the scene after Kate McCann's urgent cries for help was from the GNR. After a quick search of the apartment, during which no open bedroom window was recorded in a report, the officer initially refused to accept the parents' conviction that their daughter had been abducted and insisted she had probably managed to open a door and had wandered from the apartment and would be found walking the nearby streets. No mention had been made at this time of the open patio door.

On that basis, search parties were formed and three parties of up to twenty locals and holidaymakers combed the streets, waste-ground and the beach of Praia da Luz. In an interview with Sky News crime reporter Martin Brunt, volunteer searcher Claire Gelthorpe spoke of opening and examining the large green waste bins so familiar to visitors to Portugal and Spain to see if the child had either climbed into a bin or been dumped there after meeting a cruel end at the hand of a predatory abductor. By daylight, the search was called off.

While police concentrated their search on a child who had wandered from her bed, no warning was communicated to the border police, especially at nearby Vila Real, the closest crossing point into Spain, or to nearby ports such as Lagos or even the marine of Praia da Luz itself. Later, police would insist these alerts were sent but records showed a lapse of twenty-four hours before all border posts were officially notified of an endangered missing child.

When the Judicial Police finally arrived at the scene from their post in Portimão, the apartment was awash with people, which some estimates put at as many as twenty. These enthusiastic helpers roamed in and out of Madeleine's and the twins' bedroom, examining the open window, although none could immediately recall who had opened it or why, except the distraught Kate McCann who insisted the shutter had been down when she and her husband left to eat at the poolside tapas bar at around 8.25pm.

This type of shutter is very common in apartments and houses built after the 1970s in Mediterranean countries. It consists of a series of linked alloy or rigid plastic strips around a roller set into a box above the window and can be raised or lowered by means of a wide vertical canvas strip set into a ratchet box at the side of the window. Contrary to first reports from Praia da Luz, the shutter of the bedroom window at apartment 5A had not been jemmied open from the outside – a supposition circulated before it was revealed that the rear patio door had been left unlocked for the convenience of checking the children – but had been opened from *inside* the room. In fact, the bedroom shutter showed no sign of internal or external damage. Thus, the much-bandied question surrounding the possible drugging of the children – why did they not wake up or anyone hear the shutter being forced? – was immaterial because it hadn't happened.

Police dogs called in immediately to track the child's assumed path from the apartment actually reported following a scent to an apartment and small supermarket 400 metres away but the assumption was that the child was somewhere in the street and the premises were passed by, at which the dogs lost the scent. Could Madeleine have wandered that far before being found by her abductor? It's possible.

By daybreak, detectives from Portimão added to the crush and confusion in and around the apartment, dispatched to the scene by their regional chief Guilhermino da Encarnação. They would report back to their chief inspector in charge, DCI Amaral. In contrast to Paulo Rebelo, the bespectacled, quietly spoken deputy who would later be drafted in from

Lisbon because of his expertise in paedophilia-related investigations, Gonçalo Amaral is a detective of the old school. With the chubby cheeks of a Renaissance cherub, moustachioed, blustering and overbearing, Amaral has a tendency to quickly form his own conclusions in a case and is seldom shaken from his convictions, which in this case would be fuelled by suspicions that the McCanns and their dinner companions were not telling the whole story, as indeed it would later emerge.

Amaral had been deputy investigator to Encarnação during the search for another missing child, Joana Cipriano, who disappeared from her home in the village of Figuiera on 12 September 2004. That case ended in the conviction of Leonor and João Cipriano, the missing child's mother and uncle, although a body was never found. Accusations were made at the time that Leonor Cipriano was tortured during interrogation to extract a confession, a fact that would come back to haunt DCI Amaral later on in the McCann investigation. Cipriano confessed to killing her daughter and disposing of her dismembered body – but only after two days and nights of relentless interrogation. The following day, she retracted her confession, claiming to have been tortured and beaten.

Photographs taken after the interrogation by the Portuguese press showed the missing child's mother with extensive bruising to her arms and upper body. Both eyes were closed and swollen; her face bore yet more bruising. The police claimed she had thrown herself down a flight of stairs. DCI Amaral and four other detectives would later be charged with offences relating to the interrogation of Leonor Cipriano.

Sra Cipriano's lawyer confirmed Gonçalo Amaral was not present at the times of the alleged beatings but was accused of covering up for his colleagues, allegations he has strenuously denied. However, none of the accused detectives would be suspended from the Madeleine McCann inquiry or indeed from general duties. Amaral would be temporarily removed only after he made several critical comments aimed at the conduct of UK police in the McCann investigation.

No forensic evidence was sought in Praia da Luz that night, no cordon set up around the apartment, no fingerprint officer was on the scene. British police later called in to assist in the investigation would call the scene 'the worst preserved ever'. Most damningly, no house-to-house enquiries were made on the following day when any potential witnesses would still be in Praia da Luz. Some local apartments, many deserted during the low season, were not searched until the following Saturday, 5 May, a full forty-eight hours after Madeleine was discovered missing. Ocean Club staff would recall they were not questioned until the Sunday, when they were asked to prepare a guest list of the complex. Even then, apartments adjoining the McCanns' were never searched nor their occupants questioned and many empty properties where Madeleine may have hidden have not been searched to this day.

By now, however, DCI Amaral was moving towards his own conclusion that was to seriously damage the flow of the search. Possibly emboldened by his pyrrhic success in the

Cipriano case, the burly detective formed the opinion that the McCanns and their companions were withholding vital evidence. In fairness to the Inspector, his suspicions were founded on the unmarked shutter and the difference in times concerning the alerts to police. Kate McCann put this at ten minutes, while GNR HQ reports an alert at 11.50pm (one hour and forty minutes later).

As a possible result of the police suspicions, many standard procedures normally employed following the disappearance of a child were overlooked that night – for example, the delay in alerting border authorities, with even Portuguese police admitting to several hours' hold-up. A CCTV camera in the complex was checked and found not to be working, while another, more crucial camera covering the road from Praia da Luz to the border at Vila Real de San Antonio was never examined.

The Portuguese police were finally moved to investigate only when rumours began to circulate of a man seen taking photographs of young blonde girls on the beach in nearby Lagos, sparking tales of children stolen to order by Eastern European criminals. Police also investigated a report by a Dutch holidaymaker Andre van Wyke, who claimed that shortly after the disappearance he had seen a girl resembling Madeleine being taken in a cart to a gypsy camp near Portimão.

There would also be the discovery of a suspect vehicle near Portimão that may have been used by Madeleine's supposed abductor and a CCTV image from a petrol station near Lagos showed a child matching her description with a woman and two men. The child appeared to be arguing with the woman and the car was reported to have a British registration plate. One of the men in the CCTV footage appeared to be the one seen taking photographs of children in Lagos.

There were also some easily resolved but depressing false alarms. Police in Nelas, a mountain village of north central Portugal, thought they had cracked the case when a man was seen with a girl matching Madeleine's description in a supermarket on 8 May. He was later discovered to be a Belgian citizen who had stopped at the supermarket with his daughter.

The Dutch newspaper *Der Telegraf* published an anonymous letter intimating Madeleine's body would be found buried in foothills outside Arão, nine miles to the north-east of Praia da Luz. The search was abandoned on 15 June.

Antonio Cluny, President of Portugal's Public Prosecutors service, was moved to announce that, despite a strong conviction that Madeleine was dead, without a body the case was 'extremely complicated'. He also stressed all options, including abduction or accidental death, were still open.

Many sightings were reported elsewhere in Portugal and all of them proved to be false alarms, but there were others that would be more crucial to the investigation. All of the latter sightings, including those of Jane Tanner, Martin Smith and Gail Cooper, whose description of a man seen in Praia da Luz in the days before Madeleine's disappearance would later launch a European manhunt, seemed to have been initially ignored in favour of Amaral's infanticide theory. The chief inspector's smouldering conviction was revealed to the public on 7 May when a televised appeal to their daughter's abductor by the McCanns was followed by a police announcement stating the investigators were not '100 per cent sure' that an abduction had actually taken place.

As a result, no descriptions of Madeleine were issued by the Portuguese authorities nor posters released to request public help in the hunt, although they were later distributed by the hastily formed Find Madeleine Fund and made available for download on the Internet. Across Europe, more than a million people obliged and information began to flood in, but Portugal's somewhat eccentric laws of judicial secrecy meant no official information could be issued to the public regarding Madeleine's disappearance, although, according to a Portuguese lawyer consulted during research for this book, deviation from the secrecy laws is allowed in the 'exceptional circumstances' of missing children. While that may be so, no exception was made in the case of missing Madeleine McCann.

The Portuguese police investigation was wound down in October 2007 and the number of people working on the case reduced from a peak of 200 to just six detectives. With shifts and leaves of absence, this meant no more than three trained investigators were working on the case at any one time.

Another officer who was to appear at the forefront of the investigation as far as UK journalists were concerned was the diplomatic but harried figure of Chief Inspector Olegário de Sousa. English-speaking de Sousa was appointed press liaison officer, a position previously non-existent in Portugal where foreign reporters are directed to the number of an ethereal press office where no one ever answers the phone. Portuguese journalists, wiser in the ways of the local constabularies, resort to expense-account lunches with accommodating officers involved, usually at low level, in an investigation.

But Chief Inspector de Sousa was diplomacy personified as he met reporters for the scheduled press releases. For many months he was to serve up to the press denials of the leaks appearing in Portuguese magazines and newspapers aimed at discrediting the McCanns while speaking of 'significant' forensic information found by British teams working at the compromised crime scene. In secret, de Sousa hated the job and deplored the carefully orchestrated leaks by junior detectives to the Portuguese press. He would later ask to be removed from the case and publicly acknowledge, much to his superiors' displeasure, that the leaks were intended to push Gerry and Kate McCann into an admission that they had killed their daughter.

De Sousa also believed the case against the McCanns would not stand up in a court of law. A former colleague in the force, in whom de Sousa felt enough confidence to speak privately, revealed, 'He always insisted to his colleagues that the evidence against the McCanns was weak and would not bear scrutiny. Worse, he felt caught in the middle of a war of words between the McCann supporters and his own police force. It was not the position an honourable man would wish to find himself in.'

By the second week in May, the physical search for Madeleine McCann was all but over. Only then did the Portuguese admit to the need for assistance from the UK police specialists. Two British experts on abduction were flown in, along with a specialist team of mobile phone trackers of the type who had assisted in the investigation into the disappearance of Soham schoolgirls Holly Wells and Jessica Chapman, and helped North Wales police to locate the mysterious caller codenamed 'Phoenix' in the hunt for missing house-hunters Linda and Anthony O'Malley in Spain, in 2003.

The forensic officers from the UK conducted searches for evidence with painstaking effort. An early result was the four minuscule drops of blood found on a mosaic tile in the apartment and located by the application of luminal and hydrogen peroxide and exposure to ultraviolet light. As explained elsewhere, the blood was eventually found to be that of a male and of such a small quantity that it was hardly an indication of a crime having been committed. By this time, it was obvious the conclusion of the Judicial Police inquiry was that Madeleine McCann was dead, but it was not until the questioning of first Kate and then Gerry McCann in Portimão on 7 September that the police version of how Madeleine died became clear.

During this period, a search and forensic study was made of the Renault Scenic hired by the McCanns at the end of May, twenty-five days after they reported their daughter missing. The reasoning behind this has never been made clear since it would entail a breach of Portugal's much publicised judicial secrecy laws, but nonetheless the vehicle in which Madeleine never had the opportunity to travel allegedly revealed some forensic traces of her presence. Even if such a transfer of matter, in itself redolent of *Star Wars* technology, were possible given the vigilance under which the parents were placed from both police and international media, how they could have managed such a feat is worthy of much consideration.

Forensic testing of a boot mat removed from the car showed residues of degraded blood, body fluids and hair. Using the low-copy number DNA method described elsewhere, scientists at the Forensic Science Services laboratory in Birmingham deduced that blood, body fluid and hair matched Madeleine's DNA. We now know this laboratory method of DNA production is essentially flawed and that any of the residue found could have come from towels and clothing from the apartment where Madeleine had stayed. Despite warnings of caution from Birmingham, the news was spread by the ever-more reluctant police spokesman Olegário de Sousa.

Meanwhile, Kate and Gerry McCann, now declared official suspects, were taking a step they would have been well advised to follow as soon as the direction of the Judicial Police investigation became obvious, and had opted to return home to Rothley, Leicester.

A week after their arrival in England, a photograph taken by a Spanish tourist in Morocco was published amid speculation that the child in the photograph was Madeleine.

As the investigation appeared to stall, visits to the UK by Portuguese detectives, barred from ordering the return of Kate and Gerry McCann by their own Public Prosecutor Jose Cunha de Magalhaes, who ruled there was no new evidence to justify reinterrogation, were made to consult with colleagues in the Leicester CID. The Leicester police were unhappy with the choice of the McCanns as chief suspects and suggested a wider investigation of the circumstances surrounding Madeleine's disappearance. Criticism from the UK didn't please DCI Amaral, who went on record with a scathing criticism of the UK police, claiming they were being directed by the McCann defence team. While an unfortunate sequence of events in May 2007 may have inflamed the sensitive suspicions of Gonçalo Amaral, one wonders if the burly Faro chief inspector wasn't letting political pressure to close the case get the better of him.

Shortly after the visit by Portuguese detectives to Leicester, police spokesman Olegário de Sousa resigned from the case. This was closely followed by DCI Amaral's dismissal (he was censured for his criticism of the British police); the dismissal also followed UK press reports of his heavy drinking during lunches and the shadows growing over him and four other officers for their handling of the interrogation of Leonor Cipriano during the aforementioned investigation into her daughter's disappearance in 2004.

With Amaral returned to his desk in Faro, the local investigation came under the charge of Paulo Rebelo, who returned to old-time policing methods by ordering a search of telephone records of all calls made around the time Madeleine disappeared, hoping to discover an unusual pattern. Rebelo also appeared to be once again considering the possibility of predatory abduction when he asked for UK police help in monitoring the movements and locations of more than fifty known paedophiles with connections to the Algarve.

Within a month of his appointment as Chief Investigating Officer, the Lisbon detective was seen at apartment 5A with a team of six investigators. Together they went through various scenarios of what might have happened on the night of 3 May. All of the team members were men the newly assigned Chief Inspector Rebelo had brought down from Lisbon. They included two homicide inspectors, an officer from the Sexual Crimes Squad, another from the Robbery Squad and two specialists in technical analysis.

An examination followed of the shutters to the room where Madeleine and the twins had been sleeping and the right-hand shutter was raised to again pass through a blue blanket folded to represent the covering of a small child. DCI Rebelo appeared particularly interested in the window and was seen to raise and lower the shutter several times.

Lurking reporters perked up when the chief inspector crossed the street and looked towards Casa Liliana, the house of Robert Murat's mother, visible at a distance of 150 metres. Rebelo and one of his team then walked south towards the sea, but inquisitive Portuguese pressmen found their questions unanswered.

Within a few days, a request followed to the UK police for all paedophiles with a connection to the Algarve to be traced and questioned as to their movements around the time of Madeleine McCann's disappearance, with some speculation in the UK press as to the whereabouts of a former Praia da Luz DJ who had worked in the Plough and Harrow – an expat pub in the town that was owned by his parents Tony and Jill Ridout.

Thirty-year-old Christian Ridout, christened 'DJ Shifty' by locals, disappeared from Praia da Luz in 2005 after the mother of a twelve-year-old local girl discovered text messages to her daughter from Ridout, inviting the girl to take part in obscene sex acts. In circumstances such as these, there is always the temptation to include characters such as the unsavoury Ridout among the 'usual suspects', although a man obsessed with playing the predatory role of Humbert Humbert in Nabokov's *Lolita* isn't, according to the psychologists, in the same regressive category as paedophiles attracted to three-year-olds.

Psychologists describe paedophilia as an unnatural urge for sexual relations with children, usually aged thirteen and under, but no fine line is drawn between regressive paedophilia as defined by American psychologist James Hord, which usually involves very young children, and predatory paedophilia. Professor Hord is a psychologist in Panama City, Florida, who specialises in treating children who have been sexually abused. As described by Hord, the urge to have a sexual relationship with a young girl just entering her teens has a lot more do to with her emerging sexuality and sexual naivety than a *regressive* mental condition on the part of the male and would have to be categorised as *predatory* behaviour in the absence of regressive tendencies. In regression, Professor Hord describes the need of a sexually insecure individual to focus erotic affection on a child, thus removing the necessity for social skills in the relationship. The former he qualifies as sexual predation where the conquest of a child is seen as 'sport' and warns this part of the genre is the most dangerous of all, while the latter regressive paedophile has the urge to create a loving relationship with the child, however unacceptable that may be to society. This is not to deny the existence of those who violently assault very young children but this category, far removed from that of the regressive paedophile, contains an essence of sadism not seen in the latter.

By the end of December 2007, UK police revealed all possible suspects had been interviewed and cleared with the exception of one male, who they had still been unable to trace. A later report confirmed this man had also been traced and was able to account for his movements on 3 May. The full list of names was then passed to police in Portugal, who conducted their own checks in the area, but it seemed Madeleine's supposed abductor was not on the UK police's list of sex offenders linked to Portugal.

Although the exclusion of known paedophiles familiar with the area did not rule out the possibility of an abduction by a first-time or previously undiscovered offender, as Christmas 2007 approached the spotlight swung back to focus once more on the hapless McCanns as Rebelo announced investigators were now anxious to trace a blue tennis bag, which they claimed belonged to Gerry McCann and was now missing. No official explanation was given of the importance of the bag to the investigation.

The investigation also returned to the cemetery of Padre Pacheco's Church of Our Lady of the Light and some adjacent roadworks freshly dug just before Madeleine went missing. According to the new order established following the recent arrival of Chief Inspector Rebelo, Gerry and Kate McCann were still very much in the frame for their daughter's disappearance, and to their dismay no efforts were being directed towards the investigation of a possible abduction and a search for a live Madeleine rather than what might by now be an eight-month-old corpse.

CHAPTER 7

Early Days

In the days that immediately followed Madeleine's disappearance, Kate and Gerry McCann told the press they would remain in Portugal until their daughter was returned to them. They also publicly announced their belief that Madeleine was alive and would be reunited with her brother and sister within a few days.

Around that time, public hope also focused on the possibility that the three-year-old might have been taken by a mother who had recently lost her own child and that she would be found safe and well and returned home none the worse for the trauma. Alternatively, the worst-case scenario was that Madeleine had been taken by an out-of-town sexual predator and, being of such a young age and unlikely to be able to lead police to her abductor, would later be abandoned and found wandering by local police.

Within a few days, reports of possible sightings began to arrive in Portimão. The first was of a girl who resembled the missing child being dragged towards a boat in the marina of Lagos, 10 kilometres to the east. Another told of a small girl walking along the road with a couple acting 'suspiciously'. Two men and a woman with a blonde child were caught on CCTV at Galp petrol station on the A22 out of Praia da Luz heading east towards Spain and a girl who looked like Madeleine was seen in a red van, carrying number plates which later turned out to be false, in Lisbon.

Messages of sympathy and advice flooded in from around the world as arriving journalists, fresh from Faro airport, filed their copy over the wires. Praia da Luz and the McCann story were beginning to be big news.

In Australia, one person who would read the story and recall painful memories was Lindy Chamberlain, who knew better than most the fate that might await the McCanns. In 1980 Lindy and her husband Michael, a Seventh Day Adventist minister, told police that a dingo, the feral dog of the Australian Outback, entered their camp at Ayers Rock – a site sacred to the indigenous Aborigines and known to them as Uluru – and carried off their nine-week-old baby Azaria. The case received worldwide publicity especially when two years later Lindy Chamberlain was charged with her daughter's murder. In those days long before DNA forensic testing, the evidence presented by the Australian investigators was a bloodstained jumpsuit found near a dingo's lair. Tests by a team in London showed a blood-spatter pattern that indicated Azaria's throat had been cut, not bitten, when she was in a recumbent position, claimed by the prosecutor to be while lying in her mother's lap as in a car. Further testing of the couple's car revealed bloodstains proved to be from an infant less than six months old. Efforts appeared to have been made to wipe the blood from the car.

Lindy Chamberlain was found guilty of murdering her daughter and her husband Michael charged with being an accessory. She was sentenced to life imprisonment with hard labour. Michael received an eighteen-month sentence that was suspended for three years because it was the prosecutor's belief that he had known nothing of his wife's intention to commit the crime, although he had been guilty of helping to cover it up out of loyalty to his wife.

The case sent shockwaves around the world. Lindy Chamberlain's sentence was seen as very harsh and even senior legal experts in Australia professed doubts she had been found guilty beyond reasonable doubt. Such was the interest engendered worldwide by the story that the case had barely finished when two books hit the stands and a film was planned – named, with a certain lack of creative input, *Who Killed Baby Azaria?*

Lindy Chamberlain's lawyers appealed against her conviction and lost, but then four years after the trial a half-buried matinee jacket belonging to baby Azaria was found chewed and partially eaten outside a dingo's lair at Ayers Rock. Five days later, Mrs Chamberlain was released on the grounds that 'she had suffered enough'.

In 1988 the Chamberlains received an official pardon. At a further inquest held in 1995 the coroner returned an open verdict. In a bizarre footnote to the case, eighty-seven-year-old Frank Cole came forward in July 2004, saying he shot the dingo carrying baby Azaria on the night she went missing but did not tell anyone for fear he would be prosecuted. He said one of his friends buried the child's body. No charges were subsequently brought against him.

An assessment of the trial in legal circles concluded the reason Lindy Chamberlain was seen to be guilty in the eyes of many Australians was that she was simply perceived to be 'different'. Many Australians took a dislike to her as a mother for leaving her baby unattended in a place of danger – the area around the campsite carried warnings of wild dingoes – and wanted to see her punished regardless of the truth. A leading Australian jurist summed up public opinion: 'There is no doubt that, if Australia had capital punishment at the time, public pressure to kill Lindy Chamberlain would have been enormous.'

But it was early days for the McCanns, although criticism of the parents who left their children unattended in an unlocked apartment while they went out to dinner was beginning to surface. Nonetheless, the couple were not short of support or friends. One of the first arrivals in Portugal was Father Paul Seddon from Liverpool, who had married them in his church of Our Lady of the Compassion in Formby, near Liverpool, and baptised Madeleine. Others were family members. Gerry McCann's sister Philomena and his brother John were quick to offer support and assistance, as were Gerry and Kate's respective parents, the widowed Eileen McCann in Glasgow and Susan and Brian Healey in

Liverpool. Friends from the UK were in constant touch and often the McCanns were seen making their way down to the Church of Our Lady of the Light at the end of the Avenida de Pescadores near the beach, where they were comforted by Padre José Pacheco, the amiable parish priest.

Sympathetic too were the local uniformed police, who were not yet aware of Portimão's suspicions and were treating this as a case of a missing child, not to mention the Portuguese locals to whom the loss of a child was catastrophic.

Meanwhile, plans were made for a high-profile media blitz, which started with a simple televised appeal for the return of Madeleine, in which Gerry McCann spoke impassively about their missing daughter and his and his wife's sense of guilt at leaving their child at risk. Beside him, clutching her daughter's Cuddle Cat favourite toy, sat an apparently bemused Kate, her distraught expression as she made her own fumbling appeal to her daughter's abductor one to capture the hearts of mothers everywhere. Some small comment regarding Gerry McCann's apparent lack of emotion was made by both countries' media representatives but the McCann camp were quick to point out that the parents had been warned by police not to show emotion before the camera.

As May slipped into June with no apparent progress in the case, the McCanns became household names according to one of Britain's best-known PR gurus Max Clifford, who added it was obvious 'everyone's got their view of them'. As the days went by and weeks turned into months, his words became more and more true. The public were now witnessing a long-running middle-class soap opera that they had expected to be happily concluded within a month. While the continued disappearance of Madeleine made for an enthralling story, the McCanns' role as constantly grieving, often-photographed parents was becoming something of an irritation if not a bore. Other parents suffered similar fates without such a glare of publicity, so what was all the fanfare about? The fate of Madeleine now seemed to play a secondary role to media interest, culminating in a show of crass media vulgarity when a certain UK redtop suggested to the undoubtedly attractive Kate McCann that she should don a bikini and romp on the beach with her twins Sean and Amelie for 'some publicity shots'. Mrs McCann refused.

By now, the public were uncertain what to make of the McCanns and uncomfortable with the media campaign they had unleashed. More to the point, many public critics felt the McCanns' decision to remain in Portugal was a ruse to stay in their own share of the limelight rather than an uninspired decision to assist in the hunt for Madeleine, already firmly underway with the Find Madeleine Fund and the assembling Team McCann, currently composed of friends and relatives who were working in cramped conditions with a borrowed fax machine, answering telephones and seeking patronage and funding from celebrities who might be moved to support the campaign. Some of those celebrities responded immediately, among them family man and football star David Beckham, and others joined later as donations approached £2.3 million.

Later, the news emerged that the McCanns had used part of the Fund's reserves to make two mortgage payments on their Rothley home, which did little to help their image. In the minds of a critical portion of the public, they were seen to be cashing in on their own daughter. The residents of Praia da Luz, however, seemed content with their newfound celebrities and the tourism-orientated community under Mayor Manuel Domingues Borba were often seen lining the streets and clapping as the McCanns walked hand in hand to pray at Padre Pacheco's nearby church.

Eventually, the couple were forced to move from apartment 5A, which they continued to occupy free of charge, courtesy of Mark Warner Holidays, when the owner – a Ms Ruth McCann (no relation) of Liverpool – decided she wanted to use it for a holiday. After a brief hunt around Praia da Luz, they found an alternative villa, where they were joined by some family members and friends and they took the step of hiring a car to allow them the freedom to visit the Judicial Police HQ in Portimão, where previously they had relied on transport supplied by friends. The hire vehicle – a silver Renault Scenic – would later become a kingpin in the investigation and the source of a particularly gory theory to emerge from Portimão concerning the disposal of Madeleine McCann's corpse.

CHAPTER 8

Kate and Gerry McCann

Before Kate and Gerry McCann achieved public notoriety as prime suspects in the disappearance of their three-year-old daughter Madeleine, they were a contented, well-off young couple in their late thirties and parents of three children: Madeleine, and the younger twins Sean and Amelie.

Glasgow-born Gerry McCann was a respected consultant cardiologist at Leicester's Glenfield Hospital and a golfing fanatic, who spent many happy hours improving his handicap at Rothley Park in Westfield Lane, Rothley, close to where he and his young family lived in a four-bedroom detached house in the Leicestershire village

Rothley, pronounced 'Rowthley', is a civil parish within the Charnwood borough of Leicestershire, located just short of one kilometre west of the River Soar and eight kilometres north of the city of Leicester. The village enjoys an affluent population of 3,612 inhabitants.

Rothley is centred around the now-urbanised ancient green known as Cross Green and the Town Green, a more spacious area complete with village cricket pitch. Both are reached by a road leading from the Crossroads, which lies on the old route of the A6, now bypassing the village. The Ridgeway, an avenue of £1 million-plus houses complete with private tennis courts and swimming pools to the east of the village, has been identified in the *Sunday Times* as the most expensive place to live in England. The avenue is separated from the McCanns' home in The Crescent by a large expanse of farmland crossed by the A46.

The village is served by an arts and crafts shopping area named Woodgate, a chic centre of commerce where the visitor is spoiled for choice among antique and gift shops, and coffee and sandwich retreats as well as convenience stores. The village railway station also enjoys fame among trainspotters and railway enthusiasts, having been used to film period dramas such as the 2004 TV adaptation of Agatha Christie's *4.50 From Paddington*, when the station stood in for Paddington. It also appeared in the 1988 film *Buster*, recreating the story of the 1963 Great Train Robbery which actually took place near Ledburn in Buckinghamshire.

Most of the village children attend Rothley Church of England School but Madeleine's Catholic parents enrolled her at the Bishop Ellis Catholic Primary School in nearby Thurmaston, where the pupils reserved a special chair for Madeleine, who should have started in her Four Plus class at the beginning of the autumn term on 31 August 2007.

Head teacher Gail Neill arranged for a candle to be kept burning at the school as 'a symbol of our hope and prayers and her spirit'. She said the candle would continue to burn until Madeleine returns to blow it out herself.

Although much of the area is now carved up into expensive properties bordering a £1 million price tag in the real-estate agents' books, Rothley has its place in the Domesday Book as land belonging to the king. The area has been inhabited since Saxon times, evidenced by an ancient Saxon cross that now stands in the graveyard of the fourteenth-century Anglican parish church of St Mary and St John. Apart from being the formerly quiet countryside village thrust into the public limelight by the disappearance of little Madeleine McCann, Rothley had earned its own notoriety in the Middle Ages when it was home to a manor of the Knights Templar known as Rothley Temple. Many of the reporters with a fatherly editor or a more generous expense account have slept at the Templar manor, now refurbished and rechristened the Rothley Court Hotel.

An early owner of the Templar estate, ceded to his family in the sixteenth-century dissolution of the monasteries, was Thomas Babington, a leading Anglican evangelical who worked closely with William Wilberforce on the Bills to abolish the slave trade, an issue that would colour the disappearance of one of the village's youngest residents 200 years later.

More recently, Rothley made news in the cricketing world in 1988, when the then England captain Mike Gatting was accused in the tabloids of off-field improprieties with a barmaid at the Rothley Court Hotel. Though fiercely denied and never proven, the rumours led to Gatting being sacked from the team. But it was the events of 3 May 2007, over 1,000 miles away in the eastern Atlantic seaboard resort of Praia da Luz, that would overshadow the Knights Templar and the reported romps of an alleged cricketing Lothario when Madeleine McCann disappeared from her bedroom a week before her fourth birthday.

Now the village square is decorated with yellow ribbons, teddy bears, notes and cards from those wishing to show their support. Gerry and Kate McCann returned to Rothley in September 2007, four months after they suffered the tragedy of their daughter's loss in Portugal. Naturally, the burgeoning and obtrusive media presence in the Leicestershire village has led to inevitable tension between journalists and the local community. The majority of villagers decline to be interviewed by the press and the welcoming face of the village has changed. The strain is equally apparent for the McCanns, whose prime objective must be the welfare of their remaining children, the twins Sean and Amelie, now the centre of unthinking focus by the press corps.

Kate McCann, née Healey, was born in Liverpool, the familiar Merseyside twang still evident but now softened in her speech. She trained as a gynaecologist and anaesthetist before giving up those specialities to become a part-time general practitioner to allow her time to raise the large family for which she and her husband hoped so fervently.

The couple first met in Gerry's hometown of Glasgow, where Kate was employed at the Western Infirmary after studying medicine at the University of Dundee. Gerry attended Holyrood Roman Catholic Secondary School at Crosshill on Glasgow's Southside – reputedly the largest school in Europe with over 2,000 pupils and 150 teachers – and later studied at Glasgow University. Kate Healey was destined to continue her studies in New Zealand while Gerry had plans for Canada. However, Cupid and fate were to take a hand.

Hopelessly smitten by this tall, elegant blonde with her mischievous smile and engaging sense of humour, the young Gerry McCann was devastated at the thought of so many miles separating them after fate had brought them together. One night over a drink with Kate, he told her seriously that he was abandoning his plans for Canada. As she strove to take in the import of his news, which could have meant his decision to leave medicine, his handsome face broke into a wicked smile.

'It's just that I've met the girl of my dreams,' he told her. 'So, I'm not going to Canada – I'm going to New Zealand!' She was delighted.

Working and studying close to each other in New Zealand, the impetuous romance blossomed. In 1996, now qualified in their chosen professions, they moved back to England. Committed Catholics, they were married in church from the home of Kate's parents Brian and Susan Healey in Liverpool two years later. Gerry's widowed mother Eileen still lives in Glasgow. He and his new bride were both thirty-one, with no inkling of the cruel blow that fate was to deal them eight years later.

After their marriage, the large family that Kate had dreamed of proved difficult for the couple to achieve. Understanding the procedure as doctors and feeling that children were essential to their marriage, the young couple risked the censure of the Catholic Church and turned to in vitro fertilisation (IVF).

In vitro fertilisation is a technique in which egg cells are fertilised by sperm outside the woman's womb. *In vitro* simply refers to the glass receptacle in which the sperm is introduced to the egg. The fertilised egg is then replaced in the woman's uterus with the intention of establishing a successful pregnancy.

After several attempts at IVF and weeks of anxious waiting, the process worked and nine months later, after six years of marriage, the couple welcomed Madeleine into their lives. Kate recalls holding her newborn daughter for the first time. 'She was so small and beautiful,' she remembers, 'just like a little doll.' And so she was.

Kate had often spoken of the despair she felt on seeing friends with their children but never ceased to add how delighted she was for each little family. She knew IVF wasn't everyone's choice and that it was also frowned on by the head of her church in Rome, but she was determined to try it for herself. She recalls her happiness at Madeleine's birth: 'There she was – perfect. She was lovely; she had the most beautiful face. I thought I was going to have a boy just based on instinct. That actually made it even more special that she was a girl. She took us by surprise.'

For the first eighteen months of her young life, Madeleine was brought up in the couple's new home in Amsterdam, where Gerry studied heart-scanning techniques and continued to improve his knowledge of cardiology, while working towards his goal of a consultancy in his chosen field. It was in Holland in 2005, a year after the birth of Madeleine, that in vitro fertilisation again proved successful and Kate found herself pregnant with the twins Sean and Amelie. The McCanns' life seemed complete; neither of the doting parents could possibly have imagined the tragedy that awaited their small family two years later in a land far removed from their home.

The McCanns returned to England in that year, moving to Rothley, Leicestershire, to be nearer Kate's family. In Leicester, Gerry McCann found work at Glenfield Hospital and it was at this stage that Kate decided to give up her intended career as an anaesthetist and gynaecologist to work part-time as a GP to allow her more time for her career as a young working mother of three demanding children.

Friends and family speak of the McCanns as well-balanced working parents with an intelligent view of their responsibilities. Gerry McCann's boss at Glenfield, Dr Douglas Skehan, describes them as having 'everything you would want for. They were both successful in medicine and were able to rise to good positions. They had a family and a settled situation –' at this point, he shakes his head in incomprehension at life's vagaries '– and suddenly everything is turned into a nightmare.' It certainly appears that, had Portuguese investigators spoken to friends and family of the McCanns before considering their pressured theory relating to Madeleine's disappearance, they might well have withheld their impulsive verdict.

The question remains: were Madeleine and the twins proving too much for Kate McCann to handle as a working mother, as has been implied by Portuguese newspaper reports leaked by police with access to her diary? Kate has allegedly written that Madeleine's 'excessive activity' exhausted her. The leaks also mentioned remarks that the children were at times 'hysterical' and 'difficult to control'. What working mother, having witnessed her toddler's tantrum when refused the right to plunder a shelf of sweets and chocolate in the supermarket, might not have been capable of writing the same? In any event, the allegations of the Portuguese police have been denied by those who know Kate McCann best: a very close friend has described her as completely at ease with motherhood, a mother who loves her children and takes everything in her stride – 'So calm it's fine, with no air of negativity about her.' As a couple, the McCanns are praised as 'two special people who love their children dearly and are incapable of harming a single hair on their heads'. Nonetheless, as the investigation picked up apace following the intervention of UK police in September 2007, the Portuguese investigators remained singularly unimpressed and prepared to fly officers to Leicester to seek answers to 'crucial questions' from the McCanns and their friends at the tapas bar.

Perhaps the last words here should remain with Kate McCann's uncle Brian Kennedy, not to be confused with their millionaire supporter of the same name, who told a CNN reporter, 'You have to keep focused, and the focus is Madeleine and getting Madeleine back, and we still believe Madeleine is alive somewhere.

'We don't know who's taken her or why; we have all sorts of theories. The police in Portugal have been saying for some time they think she's dead. And they've moved from that to these fatuous allegations that one of her parents has done something. It's so ludicrous, it's beyond words.'

CHAPTER 9

First Suspect

The day following Madeleine McCann's disappearance was a Friday. Polícia Judiciária (PJ), the investigative branch of the national police force that would be involved in the investigation, immediately deployed canine handlers with tracker dogs in the wooded areas surrounding the town. There was no particular path to follow, no sightings had been reported at that time of persons loitering near apartment 5A or even shadowy figures holding a blanket-wrapped form and striding towards the dark and deserted beach.

It was logical to use tracker dogs at this early stage in the investigation. These animals are trained to follow a live scent and there were plenty of sources of the missing child's body scent to give to the animals. Unlike the 'corpse dogs' that would later be brought into the search by UK police, tracker dogs are not perceptive to the scent of decomposing organic matter as in the case of a dead body. To be more accurate, they are trained to ignore such distractions because, when working in an open environment, they are bound to come across the remains of wild animals killed by predators. Instead, they work from a 'source scent' provided by a sample of the missing person's clothing. Equally, such highly trained animals can also work from a scent left by an intruder.

The press would later fix its attention on a soft toy dubbed 'Cuddle Cat' by the missing child. According to her mother, the toy was a firm favourite and Madeleine insisted it always accompanied her to bed. Yet following her disappearance it was apparently found on a shelf in the room where Madeleine slept, placed at a height that would have been impossible for the toddler to reach. It would seem unlikely the toy had landed there in a kind of magic bullet trajectory on being thrown by Madeleine herself, although surprisingly this was one police theory. Could it be more likely that an intruder carefully placed it out of the way so as not to awaken the sleeping child before lifting her from the bed? Whatever the correct theory, the toy was never examined for DNA residue by forensic officers.

Should an intruder have been present in the McCanns' apartment, without doubt there would have been many sources of intruder DNA available to forensic scene of crime officers (SOCOs), had they had been called in before the scene of the crime was compromised. Even Chief Inspector Olegário de Sousa, the police press liaison officer brought into the investigation, was fiercely critical of the presence of so many people in the apartment throughout that first night.

In an eerie insight of déjà vu that would return to haunt all concerned, de Sousa later announced that this could have proved 'fatal' to the investigation.

Residents from the resort also joined in the hunt set in motion by Judicial Police Chief Inspector Gonçalo Amaral, fresh in from Faro. His spokesman, DCI de Sousa, was an elegant, slender man with a permanently preoccupied expression. Over the coming weeks, he would be harried by the UK journalists, already arriving in droves along with television crews comprised of sound men, cameras and presenters as word of an angelic British toddler missing on the Algarve broke on the UK morning news programmes.

The story had all the necessary ingredients to assuage the media hunger: a pretty and engaging missing child with good-looking, middle-class parents, an exotic holiday setting and local residents who spoke English and weren't camera-shy. Far from it, the arriving media found a swarm of expats anxious to get their fifteen minutes of fame before the TV cameras and equally keen to spell out their theories on the child's disappearance.

One such resident was Anglo-Portuguese real estate agent Robert Murat, a thirty-four-year-old divorced male, who lived with his seventy-one-year-old mother Jennifer in a villa located not 150 metres from the apartment where Madeleine disappeared.

Robert Murat was born at Queen Charlotte's Hospital in Hammersmith on 20 November 1973 to the late John Queriol Murat, a Portuguese company director, and Jennifer Murat, née Everleigh, formerly of Sidmouth, Devon. At the time of his birth, Murat's family lived in Richmond on Thames in Surrey but later moved to Portugal, where their son was educated and learned the language of his father with ease. This bilingual attribute would stand him in good stead working as an interpreter for Norfolk police on investigations among the wide Portuguese community when, as a young man, he returned to England in 1993, where he worked on the Bernard Matthews estate and at Inchcape Autoparc used-car dealership until 2000. It was during this time that he suffered the damage to his right eye in a motorcycle accident and this was to become a damning point of identification seven years later in Praia da Luz.

A year later Murat married Dawn Chapman in Deerham, Norfolk, and the couple lived with Dawn's son by a previous marriage, David, now twenty, and their new daughter Sofia in a semi-detached three-bedroom house in Hockering, Norfolk until they decided to move the family to start a new life in Portugal in 2002. This was shattered after just a few months when a homesick Dawn opted to return with their daughter to her family in Norfolk.

Murat chose to remain in Portugal and the breakdown of the marriage swiftly followed. His blonde four-year-old daughter, who Murat describes as his 'life', is said to bear a strong resemblance to Madeleine McCann, something that could possibly be said of most blonde four-year-old girls everywhere.

Like most expats in Portugal and Spain who know the country and speak the language, Murat drifted towards casual work in the property market, scanning newspaper advertisements and then finding buyers for the advertised property, for which he would seek a commission or introduction fee from both buyer and vendor. Alternatively, having seen what the vendor wished for the sale of the property, he would advertise it for a higher price on his own property website with a view to keeping the cash difference as a commission.

At the time of Madeleine's disappearance, he was on the point of starting his own Internet property agency partnered by his German girlfriend, thirty-one-year-old Michaela Walczuch – a married woman who lived in nearby Lagos with her pool-cleaner husband, Luis Antonio, and their eight-year-old daughter.

The new property agency – to be called Romigen, the name Murat said was formed by the first syllables of Robert, Michaela and Genesis – was set up on the Internet with the help of a Russian acquaintance Sergei Malinka, an IT specialist who would also be questioned by police concerning a long mobile telephone conversation registered between the two men close to midnight on the night of 3 May.

As a bilingual expat, Murat often worked for local police as a translator in cases involving English-speaking tourists. In fact, it would later be revealed that he had acted in the role of interpreter for the Portuguese police during their questioning of two of the McCanns' dinner companions, now dubbed the 'tapas seven' by the ever-epigraphic UK press. Journalists at the scene reported Murat's obvious desire to help, even admitting to being slightly overwhelmed by the man's passionate interest in the case. Some went so far as to remark on his constant presence at the compromised crime scene, where he was often observed to be engaging officers in conversation inside the apartment of 5A. Meanwhile, the search of the surrounding countryside went on and the investigation was now fuelled by reports of sightings of cars and strangers, the latter always acting suspiciously, in the area of the apartment on the night Madeleine went missing. Interestingly, some of those sightings were reported in statements taken from four of the McCanns' companions.

Mystery surrounds Robert Murat's whereabouts on the night Madeleine went missing. He insisted to police that he remained in Casa Liliana, the villa owned by his mother, throughout the whole of that evening. However, there were those who would dispute his story. Certainly, three of the 'tapas seven' – Fiona Payne, Rachael Oldfield and Russell O'Brien – were confronted with Murat during a police interview on 11 May and all of them identified him as the man they saw hanging around the McCann apartment between 10.30 and 11pm.

Murat's girlfriend Michaela Walczuch also came under fire from various witnesses. A Portuguese lorry driver told investigators he saw her driving a hire car on a road near the town of Silves, 40 kilometres from Praia da Luz on 5 May, when he also witnessed her hand over a child (whom he believed to be Madeleine McCann) wrapped in a blanket to a man in a black car. The sighting of Madeline in Morocco on 15 June also identifies Walczuch as being nearby moments after a child resembling Madeleine was seen with a woman in a Muslim headscarf. Walczuch herself is adamant these sightings are all untrue, claiming that on 15 June she was in conference with Murat and his lawyer, Francisco Pagarete.

Further reported sightings of Murat on the night of 3 May followed. Dr Payne and Mrs Oldfield claim they again saw him at the Ocean Club complex as late as 11.45pm. Another of the McCanns' holidaying group, Russell O'Brien, also recalls seeing the man with dark wavy hair and a distinctive lazy eye at the complex that night, with his statement allegedly confirmed by a Mark Warner employee now identified as childminder Charlotte Pennington.

As late as the end of December 2007, reports of sightings of Robert Murat near the McCanns' apartment on that fateful night continued to arrive at the Judicial Police HQ in Portimão when two British tourists who holidayed in Praia da Luz in May 2007 reported they had told the Leicester police of seeing Robert Murat in the area of the Ocean Club complex at 10.30pm, half an hour after Mrs McCann raised the alarm that her daughter was missing. Even more ominous was their recollection of seeing two men, who appeared to be watching the area from the window of an unoccupied apartment overlooking the tapas bar in the days before Madeleine vanished.

It should be noted that there was no reason whatsoever why Robert Murat shouldn't have been among members of the public gathered near apartment 5A after Madeleine McCann was reported missing; indeed, given his role as part-time police interpreter, this was even more likely. However, the die was already cast and Murat was given the status of *arguido* (declared person of interest) in May. The reports placing him at the crime scene on 3 May 2007 now numbered eight. His mother Jennifer still supports his alibi of a quiet evening spent at home in her company. Murat himself claims he knew nothing of Madeleine's disappearance until he received a telephone call from his sister in England the following morning.

Should Robert Murat have been in the area of the complex that night? Strangely, in the face of his many protests there is no reason why not – as I have already mentioned, he was often employed by the local police as an interpreter and it would seem likely that, having heard of the tragedy – Praia de Luz is, after all, a small village – he might have made his way to the complex to see if his services were required. Why should he then go to such great pains to deny he ever left Casa Liliana?

Having produced no positive results, the searches were halted on 11 May. Meanwhile, police examined photographs taken by holidaymakers in the hunt for identifiable suspects, although no clear motive for taking the child had been put forward. At this time, under area chief Gonçalo Amaral, the Judicial Police (the equivalent of the UK's CID) were pursuing two theories and relevant lines of investigation: abduction by an international paedophile network or by an illegal adoptions agency and the involvement of Gerry and Kate McCann.

What seems to have been overlooked at that time by the star-struck Portuguese police was the possibility Madeleine might have been taken by a local intruder in a crime of opportunity, not linked in any way to the international kidnapping scene. It is difficult to imagine why international criminal operatives – if they were planning to kidnap a child for a wealthy sponsor in some far-off country – should choose Praia da Luz as their base of operations, unless a local had told them of a child ripe for kidnapping because of the observed lack of security – which would have called for a large number of events to have occurred over a short period of time. Nevertheless, for an organised group to do so in the low holiday season makes it even more unlikely. Equally, the small Algarve resort would have been an unattractive venue for international paedophiles, who would have been far more likely to prowl the soon-to-be crowded resorts of Spain's nearby Costas than to chance the slim pickings on offer in Portugal in early May.

Self-confessed paedophiles to whom I talked while researching this book – an investigative journalist's lot is not always a happy one – also spoke deprecatingly of the idea of kidnapping a three-year-old for morbid sexual practices, pointing out that such a small child would only appeal to a limited few – shades here of Dr Hort's regression theory – and would have no value in the perverted marketplace of commercial paedophilia.

Again, a far more likely possibility is that Madeleine left the apartment of her own accord by the route left open to her and from there, not the bedroom, begins the mystery of her fate.

However, the Portuguese investigators were moving in an entirely different and far less logical direction. Lori Campbell of the *Sunday Mirror*, possibly sensing a scoop of the nature of the Soham murders where perpetrator Ian Huntley openly and often irritatingly expressed a desire to assist in the investigation, reported Murat's behaviour to the case investigators.

At their wits' end to solve the disappearance of a child belonging to foreign tourists in a popular holiday resort, the politically pressurised Portuguese police were more than happy to find an equally foreign scapegoat. At 7am on 14 May, a contingent arrived at Casa Liliana, the villa Robert Murat shared with his mother, and sent in the search teams. Gardens were dug over and at 4pm, as helicopters hastily hired by the press hovered overhead, police drained the swimming pool but the drained pool revealed only a plastic sandal lost by Murat's mother Jennifer a month earlier. Despite protests from those who knew him in the town, Robert Murat was held and questioned at the main police station in nearby Portimão.

Gaynor de Jesus, a former classmate and a local, who was fast logging up airtime on UK television, told reporters she was 'shocked' by Murat's apparent arrest based on his reported presence at the crime scene. 'I only know that he has been an official translator for police,' she told the gathered hacks.

Murat told police the reason for his avid interest in the case was that he had recently lost custody of his own four-year-old, who looked like the missing Madeleine. Nonetheless, he was declared an *arguido* by the police on 15 May 2007, just a few days after the McCanns admitted to the unlocked patio doors. It seemed the Portimão investigators were spoiled for choice...

It is possible Murat himself or, indeed, his solicitor asked for the *arguido* status to be declared. This category of witness has been wrongly defined by the British press as pertaining to a definite suspect (*sospieto* in Portuguese). Nor does it signify an accused person, categorised as an *acusado*. In Portuguese *arguido* is an archaic legal term formed from the barely used verb *arguir* that represents legal argument of proof. It is best defined as a status that allows the holder extra rights above those of a simple witness and also offers police a set procedure for interrogation with a lawyer present.

By law, an *arguido* is not required to answer questions that he or she feels may incriminate him or her and can legally invoke the right to remain silent during questioning. A citizen of the USA may see this as an invocation of the Fifth Amendment bestowed by the State. Above all else, it does not signify a tangible proof of guilt, as was widely reported when it was applied to Gerry and Kate McCann on 7–8 September.

The law provides detailed guidelines covering all aspects of arrest and custody. Under the law, an investigating judge determines whether an arrested person should be detained, released on bail or released outright. A person may not be held for more than forty-eight hours without appearing before an investigating judge. Investigative detention is limited to a maximum of six months for each suspected crime. If a formal charge is not filed within that period, the detainee must be released.

In cases of serious crimes such as murder or armed robbery, or of those involving more than one suspect, investigative detention may last for up to two years and in extraordinary circumstances can be extended by a judge to three years. A suspect in investigative detention must be brought to trial within eighteen months of being formally charged. If a suspect is not in detention, there is no specified period for going to trial: a detainee has access to lawyers and the government assumes the cost, if necessary.

There was no way the Portuguese police were going to allow their recently arrived diversion to escape them. Chief Inspector de Sousa had already complained tersely about the ruined crime scene at 5A, telling the press that this had seriously complicated the work of the scientific team and may even have destroyed all evidence – a situation that could prove fatal to the investigation. The mild-mannered chief inspector was obviously lining up his force's guns in defence of the criticism that was to come, for the negligence in failing to secure the original crime scene was down to his department alone. Now the police had Robert Murat, delivered to them by the same British press criticising their investigation. And, despite his protests that he was being made a scapegoat, two other people linked to him would soon find themselves in the Portimão interviewing room.

CHAPTER 10

The Russian Connection

Russian national Sergei Malinka was a twenty-two year-old IT specialist who had set up a website for Murat's property agency business. Apparently the suspicion soon to be aimed at Malinka was based on the fact that he and Murat had exchanged frequent telephone calls in the days since Madeleine's abduction. A computer was seized from the Murat villa and a laptop and hard drives taken from Malinka's workspace but investigation spokesman DCI de Sousa told journalists there was insufficient evidence to make any arrests.

The Russian also came under fire from the Portuguese media, which seemed characteristically unfazed by possible libel actions.

Meanwhile, Malinka was interrogated in a five-hour interview at the main police station in Portimão. There, he denied all reported contacts with Murat, insisting he had not spoken to the man in over a year, a statement later disproved when police unearthed Murat's mobile phone records that allegedly showed he called Malinka at 11.40pm on the night of Madeleine's disappearance.

Perhaps given the suspicions surrounding Robert Murat at that time, the Russian might be forgiven for distancing himself from any suggestion of friendship, but inconsistencies in his account of his relationship with the property agent emerged. With regard to the midnight telephone call, Malinka insisted he had not contacted Murat in a year. It seemed a sense of panic had overtaken some of those questioned by the Portuguese on what happened that night. Truth, it seemed, was at a premium in Praia da Luz in the month of May 2007.

The second person to be interviewed concerning their relationship with Robert Murat was Dawn Murat, his estranged wife, who was living with their four-year-old daughter in England. Some other witnesses connected to Murat were also reinterviewed including his mother Jennifer.

Press interest focused on the real estate agent as he was again called for interview on 10 and 11 July. On the second day of the interviews, three of the McCanns' companions, who had been dining and drinking with them on the evening Madeleine went missing, were also recalled for questioning. Rachael Oldfield, Fiona Payne and Russell O'Brien were summoned to Portimão to re-examine their statements with regard to their recollections of the events of the evening of 3 May. During these interviews, they were individually brought face-to-face with Robert Murat as police investigators pointed out discrepancies between the statements of the friends and that of Murat, in particular regarding the claims of the former that they had seen the real-estate agent outside the Ocean Club complex on the night of the disappearance. Murat, it appeared, insisted he was at home with his mother at the time stated by the McCanns' dinner companions. His mother would later corroborate his alibi.

What must have struck the English trio as particularly bizarre was that in his role as a police interpreter Murat translated the original statement of both Rachael Oldfield, whose statement given at that early stage was now under re-examination, and Dianne Webster, mother of fellow diner Fiona Payne.

Murat's lawyer Francisco Pagarete would later add to the confusion by issuing a statement on behalf of his client that Robert Murat had 'also' assisted police during the interview with Dianne Webster. It seemed he was not present during interviews with 'multiple witnesses' as reported in the press and had not been employed as a translator at any other interview, while forgetting to mention that Murat also translated the statement of another holidaymaker, Bridget O'Donnell, another witness to events of 3 May.

The investigation was now approaching three months and the suspicions cast on Murat and possibly Malinka were the only relief for the now sun-bronzed hacks under pressure from their editors. Where was the text? What was the story?

Hopes brightened in early August when police search teams, this time including UK police detectives, once again turned up at Casa Liliana. Top soil and vegetation was stripped from the garden on the 4th of August, where hi-tech scanning equipment with the ability to seek out buried organic matter such as a decomposing corpse was used. Police sniffer dogs from the UK were also on hand, among them Ernie, a lively cocker spaniel whose unsociable forte was recognising the smell of decomposition.

Apart from the Murat property receiving the benefits of a good weeding, nothing untoward was found in a full day of searching. A puzzled Jenny Murat told reporters gathered at her villa's green panelled metal gates that the case against her son was 'a lot of poppycock' and the combined forces of the UK's Fourth Estate groaned as DCI de Sousa announced there was insufficient evidence to make any arrests. Murat was questioned in 2014 in a new inquiry into the case, as was his German-born wife, but he was removed from the Portuguese police's *arguido* list in 2008.

CHAPTER 11

Facing
the Media

While the investigation in Portugal rumbled on, relatives of the McCanns and interested parties got together to launch the Find Madeleine appeal, the aims of which were to find Madeleine, support the family, bring the abductor or abductors to justice and, subject to those first aims, to help other missing children.

Within a year of its inception, more than £1.3 million was received in public donations. However, and as ever, tricksters and scam artists were at work, hoping to divert cash donated to a worthy cause into their own pockets. Many of these counted on Internet users logging on to their fake webpage and registering as a hit, which meant cash from advertisers. The website appearing at the front of this book from which an excerpt of the Fund's aims has been taken is www.findmadeleine.com, the official website containing regular updates from Gerry McCann.

As the Fund and the story of the missing child gained momentum around the world, an announcement from the McCanns made it clear that the couple would stay in Portugal for 'as long as it took' to find Madeleine. Such a statement engendered huge public sympathy and the world's heart went out to the now-bereft parents. Across Europe, other parents kept an increasingly vigilant eye on their offspring and warned their children of the dangers of speaking to strangers. Of course, these dangers were real enough, but how could one guard against a child being snatched from her bed?

But for all the sympathy, recrimination against parents who would leave their young and vulnerable children in an unguarded and unlocked apartment while they dined with friends out of earshot of their brood also followed. Comments of this nature were not unexpected and no one could doubt such thoughts would be in the minds of any parents witnessing such a tragedy. The human race has a great propensity for self-righteous anger.

What most offended people reading the story, however, was the apparent acceptance of celebrity status exhibited by the McCanns – in particular, Gerry – despite a statement issued by the couple on 5 May 2007 in which they spoke of their anguish and despair at their daughter's disappearance.

Whenever the McCanns left their newly rented villa in Praia da Luz looking tanned and fit, the world's press were waiting. Cameras clicked as they made their way to church. Gerry held his wife's hand, while Kate McCann in turn clutched the rumpled Cuddle Cat, Madeleine's loved soft toy, to her chest or at times even pinned it to her handbag.

Crowds clapped in sympathy and messages of condolence and hope flowed in from world leaders.

Even at this early stage, critics of the couple complained at the world's spotlight being focused on two parents who had abandoned their child to her fate while the relatives of other missing children were ignored by the media and saw their own case files closed by police. Clarence Mitchell spent nearly a month between May and June 2007 with the McCanns in Portugal, often with them for up to twelve or fourteen hours a day, while representing the Foreign and Commonwealth Office when he held the post of director of the government's Central Office of Information's Media Monitoring Unit. He would later return as their official spokesman in September after Justine McGuinness stepped down from the role, and shortly after the declaration by Portuguese police of the McCanns' status as *arguidos* in the investigation.

Meanwhile, the McCanns were receiving spiritual comfort from the parish priest of Praia da Luz, the bespectacled and balding forty-six-year-old Padre José Pacheco in his brightly painted yellow-and-white Church of Our Lady of the Light. The amiable priest took Kate's confession on the day after Madeleine's disappearance and later gave the couple keys to the church so they could enter and pray between services. This was an act of Christian kindness that was to backfire badly when the couple were individually cited as possible suspects in the case. As the mood towards Madeleine's parents cooled, parishioners began to speak out against the priest's charitable action, which also brought him a reprimand from the Bishop of the Algarve. Portuguese investigators also brushed aside

Padre Pacheco's protestations of Holy Orders and demanded to know what the reportedly devout Kate McCann had told him in confession. True to his calling, Padre Pacheco refused to divulge the secrets of the confessional.

But despite the impending furore in Praia da Luz, the McCanns continued to be fêted abroad. On 30 May, just three weeks after Madeleine's disappearance, eighteen days after her fourth birthday and two weeks after Robert Murat fell foul of Portuguese investigators, they flew to Rome in a private jet provided by Topshop billionaire Sir Philip Green for an audience with Pope Benedict XVI.

During an emotional meeting, the Catholic pontiff took Mrs McCann's hand and promised to pray for her daughter's safe return. The trip to the Vatican was promoted by the Find Madeleine Fund as the first stop in a 'European Tour' to raise awareness of her disappearance.

Meanwhile, from Portimão, Portuguese investigators issued what they hailed as their first major breakthrough. This was a description of a man seen carrying an object 'that was a child or could have been taken as a child' on the night Madeleine went missing. The suspect was 1.78 metres tall, about 5 feet 10 inches although this was later amended to 1.70 metres (5 feet 7 inches) due to an 'error in translation'. He was aged about thirty-five with oily, dark straight hair worn to collar length and slight in build, narrowing the suspects to just about every male in the country's population over thirty years of age, around three million individuals. The coûp de grace was an Identikit of the suspect's face without features, which drew much ridicule on the hard-pressed force from the media. They were, the investigators felt, doing their best with a seemingly hopeless case.

The tide of opinion, barely voiced in public before, was beginning to turn. Both the public and the police now started to consider the possible involvement of the parents in Madeleine's disappearance. Still on their European tour, the McCanns were asked by a German reporter at a press conference in Berlin how they felt now that more and more people were pointing the finger at them. On 12 June, five weeks after their daughter disappeared, the McCanns flew back to Portugal. Five days later, DCI de Sousa made his milestone statement that vital evidence had been destroyed by the lack of forensic response in the hours following Madeleine's disappearance.

With no clues other than the description of a faceless man and a few dubious sightings at petrol stations between Praia da Luz and the Spanish border, the police were forced to look for other possible crime scenarios. Gerry and Kate McCann were moving, inexorably, into the investigators' spotlight.

CHAPTER 12

Casting the Net

Early July 2007 saw the re-questioning of Robert Murat, as mentioned earlier, and later that month the British police paraded their corpse dogs, Eddie and Keela. Eddie would root out a corpse while Keela's speciality was the detection of minute spots of blood. The possibility of abduction was now moving towards accidental death – and, more to the point for the McCanns, accidental death *en situ*. The Portuguese police now seemed intent on proving Madeleine died in apartment 5A and her body was removed and hidden for later burial by who else but their obvious suspects: the McCanns, being family and first on the scene – both entrenched police indicators of prime suspects.

So what was the theory and could it hold up to examination? According to the Portuguese, the answer is yes. Viewed logically, away from the pressure to close the casebook, it's doubtful. The police built their case on the unproven assumption that the McCanns were in the habit of tranquillising their offspring to ensure an undisturbed evening while they dined with friends. They argued that both parents were medical professionals and at least one had trained in anaesthetics. In any event, according to the police, both would have access to tranquillisers. But what the police case overlooked, and what any defence lawyer worth his fee and certainly as skilled as Michael Caplan, QC, Angus McBride and Carlos Pinto de Abrèu would pick up on, was that tests on Sean and Amelie McCann showed no sign whatsoever that either child had ever been dosed with a tranquilliser. Even more bizarre was the police theory on storage and disposal of Madeleine's body. Or are such horrific theories no more than an indication of the intense political pressure that the Portuguese police continued to be under to close the case? There is no doubt such pressure exists to solve any case of possible child abduction but the Portuguese Interior Ministry had a special interest, rather than just a wish by the Ministry of Tourism to prove that kidnapping of children is not prevalent on the Algarve. After all, children disappear much more rapidly in Africa or even while popping off to the shops in Manchester. As Cecile B. De Mille would have put it with regard to the police case: 'too much production...'

On that last point, the opinion of the less-feverish UK police called in by the Portuguese was that three-year-old Madeleine was abducted in either a crime of opportunity by a hovering paedophile, who had noted the visits to the apartments by members of the dinner party, or by a person who had observed the ritual of leaving the children unattended and the patio door unlocked during the McCanns' stay. Nor did the UK police discount the possibility of Madeleine leaving the apartment and being carried off in the street.

In his novel *The Four Signs*, Sir Arthur Conan Doyle has his famous character Sherlock Holmes pronounce: 'Take away the impossible and that which is left, my Dear Watson, however improbable, is the truth.' It isn't impossible for a child to be taken off the street, even abducted from her bed by a sexual predator then murdered and buried on a deserted beach, however improbable and unpleasant that possibility might be. But to clutter an investigation with media theories, the arrest of over-attentive interpreters and rumours of international paedophile rings operating on the Algarve or billionaire sheiks buying small companions for their spoiled children is clouding the issue into oblivion.

But the Portuguese police would go further than bizarre theories and damaging leaks to the home media to close the file on Madeleine McCann, as would be revealed in the months ahead. The truth is that, one year later, the investigation was no further on than when it began, not with a bang but with a decidedly ineffective whimper at 11pm on 3 May 2007.

The fact was that little Madeleine McCann appeared to have been taken from her bed by a person, or persons, unknown or, a more likely possibility for some reason unacceptable to Portimão, carried off while wandering the street. After that her fate was, and is still, a matter of conjecture.

CHAPTER 13

Flawed
Evidence

The Portuguese legal system was overhauled on 17 September 2007 and many cynics assume the long overdue reviews and amendments were to prove convenient for the elite of Lisbon's high society about to enter the dock in 2008 for the reopening of the Casa Pia scandal, in which orphans in the charge of the state were regularly rented out to paedophiles occupying high office in the government, police and judiciary.

Of particular interest to the McCanns' lawyers, however, was a forecast amendment to Code 86 of the Secrecy Act that currently prevented Madeleine's parents from speaking publicly about the case or lifting the veil on documents concerning their daughter's disappearance.

Code 86 prevents any witness, suspect or investigating officer revealing evidence or statements connected with the case to any person other than a colleague involved in the same inquiry. It does not even permit officers employed elsewhere to have access to the evidence.

The original raison d'être behind the code was to protect subjects of the King from scurrilous gossip, should they be interrogated by a marshal of the King's court. Sadly, as is true of all the laws of democracy, this can also be used to the advantage of the state. As such, while vague assertions of damning evidence from the police occasionally slipped into the columns of Portuguese and UK newspapers, the McCanns were forbidden, under pain of imprisonment, from discussing the case. Of course, in speaking to the press, albeit through strategically planned leaks, the Portimão investigators were equally breaking the law – but who watches the watchers in any society?

The first evidence against Gerry and Kate McCann came after the inquiry into the comings and goings of Robert Murat on the night of 3 May had been thoroughly exhausted. As detailed, Murat had been questioned along with Sergei Malinka, his Russian webmaster, gardens had been dug up and pools drained. Apart from a few hysterical reports of Murat being out and about in Praia da Luz in the hours following Madeleine's disappearance, as well he might have been as an overzealous police interpreter, there was nothing to connect him to the alleged abduction. The fact that he had a lazy eye due to a detached retina and a daughter approximately Madeleine's age back in the UK was hardly the stuff of major plots.

Gerry and Kate McCann, however, unwillingly played into the investigators' hands with their first omission concerning the patio doors. While in retrospect it is not difficult to understand their trepidation in admitting to an austere and unfamiliar authority that they regularly left their daughter and her two siblings alone in the evenings while they dined and drank with friends, nonetheless the consequence was obvious.

Not even the fact they had been made *arguidos* and given the status and privileges of 'category one witnesses' should have been made public, but it was – though by which camp no one is now certain.

In early August 2007, the dramatically leaked news that traces of blood had been found in Madeleine's bedroom by British sniffer dogs flown in from the UK gave everyone pause for thought and coincided with a police plot fostered by Detective Chief Inspector Amaral to put pressure on the McCanns through the press.

What was not made clear to the press was that the minuscule specks of blood found in the apartment were too degraded for intelligent analysis; the only result published from the Forensic Science Service in Birmingham was that the blood was from a male. In truth, this important forensic report of degradation and its relationship to Madeleine, when questioned by the more ethical members of the UK press, was denied. But blood had been found in the missing child's bedroom and that was good enough from Portimão.

The next bombshell for the McCanns was that Eddie, the black-and-white spaniel from the UK force, allegedly detected the smell of a dead body inside apartment 5A. A general tenet of forensics is that a corpse must lie for at least two hours before removal to leave enough residues to alert a trained dog.

By 21 August 2007, the jubilant investigators leaked their theory that Madeleine McCann died in the apartment. Now there was no turning back. The McCanns were declared *arguidos* and all theories of abduction, either from the apartment or from the street, were now being discounted.

Further stories in the Portuguese press – now skating dangerously close to breaking the laws on libel and calumny that eventually led to a libel action by the McCanns against the newspaper *Tal e Qual* – spoke of 'significant' results from the forensic tests carried out in Birmingham. If anyone had bothered to speak to the Birmingham laboratory, the word 'significant' would have been denied, but the Portuguese police knew they were dealing with a press corps that wouldn't let the facts spoil a good story.

After the declaration of the McCanns' suspect status on 7 September, the couple made plans to fly back to the UK and continue their campaign to find Madeleine from there. Meanwhile, the Portuguese kept up the pressure by revealing the news of their extraordinary finds from the McCanns' hire car, in which they had driven to Faro airport to start their journey home with the twins.

The story of what police allegedly found in the boot of the hire car, a Renault Scenic rented locally, would defy even the convenient logic of Portimão. Information leaked to *Correio de Manhã* and other nationals quoted a 100 per cent match to Madeleine's corpse in the Renault Scenic, indicating the child's badly decomposed corpse – imagine a joint of meat left out of the freezer for more than three weeks in temperatures approaching 25°C – had at some point been transported in the car. While the time lapse between Madeleine's disappearance and the hiring of the car by Gerry McCann was a full twenty-five days and would never have been accepted in fiction, it was good enough for DCI Amaral, who now passed the case file to the Public Prosecutor.

With such sterling and frankly miraculous results for DNA tests on the hire car, the Portuguese now requested the UK police to seize Kate McCann's diary and Madeleine's soft toy, the pink Cuddle Cat that Kate carried everywhere in the weeks following her daughter's disappearance. Kate's admission that she washed the toy because it was dirty and covered in sun lotion was put forward by Portimão as further indication of her guilt.

Throughout all the revelations of evidence descending on the Portuguese media that should have seen some form of censure and was clearly in breach of Clause 86, Gerry and Kate McCann were under strict instructions not to discuss the case or make a public rebuttal of the evidence published against them.

Something that escaped the attention of the Portuguese press – the inevitable fact that spoils a good running story and is therefore conveniently overlooked – was the announcement from the Portuguese Public Prosecutor's Office that there was insufficient evidence to reinterrogate the McCanns. Gonçalo Amaral was removed from the inquiry in October but there is no doubt that the seeds he sowed of the McCanns' involvement in the disappearance of their daughter had set the inquiry back many months, during which time the only efforts to find Madeleine alive were consigned to a Spanish private detective agency that was big on promises if more than a little short on results.

The legal amendments of September made it necessary for there to be firm evidence against a suspect before the status of *arguido* could be given, therefore following the announcement of the Portuguese Public Prosecutor that Gerry and Kate McCann, and let's not forget the equally abused Robert Murat, should have been removed from the suspect list. However logical that might seem, it was not to be and public disclosure of actual evidence held by the police was postponed for four months on both counts, meaning neither party could hope to be relieved of suspect category until mid-April 2008, if then.

Without that extension, there could have been an end to the rumour and speculation surrounding the inquiry. It would also make it more difficult for Portuguese police to tap the telephones of the McCanns and their confidants or Murat because this is only permissible and granted by a judge in the case of *arguidos*.

The couple renewed their attack on the rumours as they announced an £80,000 advertising campaign to find Madeleine and it was reported that entrepreneur Richard Branson had given £100,000 to create a fighting fund to help the McCanns clear their name.

As already recounted in Chapter 7, Lindy Chamberlain-Creighton also came to the defence of the beleaguered McCanns by claiming the public were viewing Madeleine's disappearance as a reality-TV show with no ending.

Writing in the *Mail on Sunday* in late November 2007, she declared: 'It is as if we have run over the hour allotted for the "show" and the viewers are saying: "Where's the answer?" When the public atmosphere is like this, questions of justice or truth start to take second place.'

CHAPTER 14

Blood and Fluids

By now, the Portuguese investigators were relying heavily on forensic results from UK police but they were putting their own interpretation on the results. The British police dog Keela had reacted to a portion of wall in apartment 5A and a test for blood with a luminol and hydrogen peroxide solution gave off a characteristic white-green light as the agents reacted under ultraviolet light. However, the spots revealed were minuscule, of a silhouette-and-splatter pattern that might result from shaking a minor injury or even from a distant sneeze. More to the point, neither the luminol and hydrogen peroxide solution nor other agents possibly used at the scene such as Peroxstemo, Hemident or Heglostix can differentiate between human and animal blood, which would need thorough laboratory tests to determine age, gender and blood group. The last three are conducted by a release agent being sprayed across the suspected area and either paper spills or cotton buds soaked in the reactive solution to reveal a blood trace.

Despite warnings from UK forensic officers that the findings were inconclusive, local police leaks to the Portuguese press and TV media, whose reporters were by now in a frenzy of accusations against the McCanns, failed to take into account the precautionary nature of the finds. Blood traces had been found on the wall of an apartment regularly rented out throughout the year. That was enough to start a rampage against the parents.

Not to be outdone, UK corpse dog Eddie performed dramatically when brought near the hire car rented by Gerry McCann twenty-five days after his daughter had gone missing. This time the focus of attention was the boot of the Renault. Other cars used by the McCanns and two belonging to Robert Murat and his mother were also tested without positive results.

Eddie the spaniel's excitement at the boot of the hired Renault Scenic was matched by his equal enthusiasm in areas of apartment 5A. Again, the information was dramatically leaked to the Portuguese press before UK forensic officers had a reasonable time to verify and collate their findings. No questions seemed to have been asked of the person renting the car that allegedly bore traces of Madeleine's body fluids, hair and blood on the night she disappeared. An enquiry to the car-hire company brought me into contact with a male voice that stated the company had been advised not to discuss the matter with unauthorised persons. In Portugal, that means anyone not officially involved in the investigation.

Supposing the body fluids, tissues and hair found in the boot of the Renault Scenic were from Madeleine McCann, then it would follow that her decomposing body would have been hidden for twenty-five days in a location where it would not be found in the first intensive hours of the hunt. The average weight of a three-year-old of Madeleine's McCann's stature would be between 30 and 35 pounds. The time taken for a body to decompose depends on climatic conditions such as temperature and moisture as well as accessibility to insects. Due to the profusion of insects found in southern Portugal in early summer and the normal processes of decomposition, a human body in an exposed location could be reduced to bones in just nine days.

Within four to ten days, bacteria deposited by insects have broken down tissue and cells, releasing fluid into the body cavities and the body becomes bloated from the build-up of gases produced by the bacterial invasion. These gases, including hydrogen sulphide, methane, cadaverine and putrescine, are foul-smelling but they are exactly what the corpse dog is trained to detect. Moving a body hidden in an exposed location for more than forty-eight hours would be a very unpleasant exercise and after twenty-five days it would need a very strong stomach indeed.

At the moment of death, certain chemical changes, known as autolysis, take place in the body. These are basically no more than a breakdown of tissue by the body's own chemicals quickly accompanied by the action of bacteria. Both processes release foul-smelling gases, the chief source of the odour of a dead body.

Within ten days, skin would have sloughed off the corpse, exposing yellowing flesh and 'black putrefaction' would begin. After twenty days, the corpse passes into the first stages of butyric fermentation, at which all remaining flesh will have been stripped from the body by insect activity and the bones exposed. The corpse appears flattened and dehydrated, and emits a strong, cheesy smell caused by butyric acid that attracts another suite of corpse organisms. The surface of the body in contact with the ground becomes covered in a dark mould as the body ferments.

A corpse dog operates by picking up the smell of decomposing flesh or, more correctly, by the scent of the body fluids and gases accompanying decomposition. Some of these are body fluids immediately expelled at death; others form during rigor, while the fluids of decomposition occur in bloody discharges from the nose, mouth, ears and other body orifices, even exuding from the scalp. But sadly for the Portuguese police theories, corpse or cadaver dogs are not infallible. In fact, attorneys in the Dane County Court of Wisconsin had already convinced Judge David Fielding that certain dogs were accurate only between 22 to 38 times in 100 searches.

In the case of Eugene Zapata versus State of Wisconsin (September 2007), the prosecution could only claim a success rate of 60 to 69 per cent, creating a legal precedent that could influence the case against the McCanns. The reason for the challenge against the efficiency of these highly trained dogs was that, in the case of supposed victim Jeanette Zapata, who disappeared in 1976, a body was never found and the prosecution relied heavily on the reaction of the cadaver dogs during the search of a cabinet freezer at the home she shared with her husband, the suspected killer. In the McCann case, Portimão was relying heavily on the Portuguese press, casual leaks to whom could be relied on to reach sensational proportions in the following day's headline, resulting in the McCanns launching a libel action against *Tal e Qual* concerning such unrestrained reporting.

The cause of the dogs' inaccuracy depends on the amount of time it takes for the smell of decomposition to remain once a body has been removed. Corpse (or cadaver) dogs have been known to find the remains of people who have been dead for decades but, once the remains have gone, the smell of death rapidly dissipates. If the speculation surrounding Eddie's excitement in the apartment is that Madeleine died on the night of her reported disappearance, at least three months would have elapsed. An expert army dog-handler acquaintance whom I approached while researching this book told me he wouldn't have expected the scent to last more than four weeks and added that his own dog had become excited when an overripe chicken carcass leaked into the boot of his car while on the way to the municipal dump.

As an afterthought to such speculation, chemically produced solutions or *pseudoscents* are commercially produced for training dogs. The various formulae include recently dead, post-decomposition and victims of drowning. The possibility must remain that, if something can be artificially produced in laboratories, it could equally come about by a fault of nature.

Forensic tests on the blood traces found in apartment 5A

were carried out in a Birmingham laboratory and newspapers in both the UK and Portugal picked up on the speculation that the blood was that of Madeleine McCann, although this was never confirmed by UK forensics. In a dramatic statement, police spokesman DCI de Sousa acknowledged Madeleine might possibly be dead but refused to consider the McCanns as suspects, despite pressure from the media.

On 7 September, after a day of lengthy questioning at the police HQ in Portimão, Kate McCann was declared a suspect. That afternoon her husband was awarded the same status. A meeting of the six directors of the Madeleine Fund was called within a few days and the following statement issued:

With the sudden dramatic and unexpected turn of events at the weekend the directors had to consider whether legal defence costs could be paid for by the Fund.

The Board has taken advice from Bates Wells & Braithwaite London LLP and Christopher McCall QC. The Board has been advised that payment of Gerry and Kate's legal defence costs would be legally permissible subject to conditions about repayment in the event of a guilty conviction.

The directors of the Fund discussed this today. The two family directors, Brian Kennedy and John McCann, withdrew from the meeting when the decision was made. Esther McVey chaired the meeting.

The Fund directors realise that there is not only a legal answer and recognise the spirit which underlies the generous donations to Madeleine's Fund, which it is the directors' responsibility to steer.

For this reason the Fund directors have decided not to pay for Gerry and Kate's legal defence costs. We stress that Gerry and Kate have not asked for these costs to be paid. However, people have already called in offering their financial support. Any such fund to pay legal defence costs would have to be separately set up and administered.

At the heart of this campaign and Fund is a little girl confused, lonely and in need of her parents. This Fund's money will be focused on finding that little girl and leaving no stone unturned.

Madeleine's fund is a non-charitable not-for-profit company, which has been established to help find Madeleine McCann and to support her family and bring her abductors to justice. Any surplus funds will be used to help families and missing children in the United Kingdom, Portugal and elsewhere in similar circumstances. If there are surplus funds Madeleine's Funds can be converted into a charity.

The Fund is following best practice governance procedures as set out in the Good Governance Code for the Voluntary and Community Sector. The directors of the company are Peter Hubner, Brian Kennedy, John McCann, Michael Linnett, Esther McVey, Doug Skehan and Philip Tomlinson. They have appropriate legal, business and charitable experience. An experienced

Fund Administrator has been appointed to ensure the highest standards of transparency and accountability. This should enable the Directors to maintain an appropriate governance distance in the day-to-day operations of the Fund.

The Board and its individual Directors will ensure that the Fund is subject to required financial legal scrutiny. They will ensure that they receive reliable external advice and information, as the basis for making good decisions.

CHAPTER 13

Leaving No
Stone Unturned

The announcement from local Judicial Police HQ in Portimão that Kate and Gerry McCann were now officially awarded the title of *arguido*, with the legal caveat that the title incurred, sent the European press into a feeding frenzy but the McCanns still had powerful supporters.

As far back as 12 May 2007, the day of Madeleine's fourth birthday, the couple heard that celebrities including Harry Potter author JK Rowling and Topshop billionaire Sir Philip Green had donated towards a £2.5 million reward offered for Madeleine's safe return. Even Chancellor Gordon Brown, moved perhaps by the remembered loss of his own daughter, Jennifer Jane at a few days old in 2002, sent a message of condolence and offered future help to the parents.

The two days following Madeleine's fourth birthday offered a possible breakthrough in the case when police searched the villa Robert Murat – also an official *arguido* – shared with his mother. Casa Liliana was situated a scant 150 metres from where Madeleine had been abducted. Ten days later the world prayed with the McCanns when they visited the Marian shrine of Our Lady of Fatima near Ourém, far north of the Algarve. Their confession of guilt at leaving Madeleine alone and unprotected in apartment 5A moved the hearts of many of their previous doubters.

But the words of condemnation issued by the Polícia Judiciária under Gonçalo Amaral in Portimão caused a massive about-face in public opinion. Now the theories were of drugged children, accidental death and bodies hidden in the night, fired by fertile imaginations bred on controversial theories from the Portuguese press – and the Portimão investigators seemed more than happy to provide the fuel.

But Kate and Gerry McCann were embarking on a journey that would bring controversy of its own as they determined to leave no stone unturned – the motto of the Find Madeleine Fund – in the high-profile search for their daughter. The first step in the campaign to raise awareness of Madeleine's plight was an arranged audience with Pope Benedict XVI at the Vatican. From there, the campaign plans took them on to press conferences and meetings with officials and politicians in Germany, Morocco, the Netherlands, Spain and the USA. The worldwide publicity had exactly the effect its critics had feared. Public opinion was now seeing the McCanns as a couple obsessed with publicity, openly enjoying their celebrity status won at the sacrifice of their daughter. It was a cruel verdict inflicted by a cruel world and would also bring criticism of a previous police action in Portugal surrounding Rui Pedro Teixeira Mendonça, a boy who disappeared in Lousada in 1998, fuelled by a controversial report in a UK newspaper of Portuguese border police ignoring orders for vehicle searches in the McCann investigation and remaining in their cars to wave traffic across the border simply because it was raining. The battle of the two national media, it seemed, had been joined.

Meanwhile, the desperate investigators, loath to take a step back in their accusatory campaign against the McCanns, now resorted to trawling through dossiers of emails and letters from clairvoyants and psychics. Having received criticism from police sources when I used information from a UK medium to successfully trace the body of a Swiss national murdered in southern Spain in 2001, I asked a friend to pass on my congratulations to Gonçalo Amaral on his acceptance of the esoteric in the investigation. As I expected, a grumpy reply from his office stressed detectives were merely testing the messages to see if any of them were from Madeleine's kidnapper.

Amaral's investigators were also kept busy by hundreds of tip-offs engendered by the large reward that placed Madeleine's body at various points in local scrubland surrounding the town. The £2.5 million reward was turning the search into a hunt for the Easter Bunny, with gamblers choosing sites to be searched without leaving their armchairs. Meanwhile, live Madeleines were popping up in places as diverse as Morocco, Spain, France, Switzerland, Belgium and even Argentina and Guatemala. One could almost hear the collective sighs of relief from Portimão when Gerry and Kate McCann were finally elected as prime suspects.

Others less convinced of their guilt attempted to extort money from the family with false promises of key information for cash and one such fraudster and his female companion were eventually arrested in Spain. Another arrest was made in the Netherlands.

By early August, a month before the McCanns would receive suspect status, Belgian police conducted a search in Tongeren for a couple seen with a girl resembling Madeleine. Portuguese police had by now returned to Casa Liliana and were digging up Mrs Murat's garden.

It was at this time, early August 2007, that it became even more apparent to observers that the Portuguese press were launching a deliberate smear campaign against the McCanns and their companions from the tapas bar. Protests by the McCanns' spokeswoman Justine McGuinness led the UK press, feeling they'd been left on the sidelines, into baying for the blood of officers who were leaking disinformation to the Portuguese media. The McCanns, meanwhile, continued their daily prayers for their daughter at the nearby Church of Light, whose pastor, Padre Pacheco, was soon to be dragged into the controversy as the suspect couple's confessor.

A fact kept from the public at this time was that the results of the DNA tests on small blood spots found in apartment 5A by Keela, the British police dog, positively revealed the gender to be male. Instead, much was made of Keela's work companion, the cadaver hunter Eddie, detecting a 'body scent' in the same area. The Portuguese press were delighted to pass the selective snippet on, together with the 'off-the-record' message from Portimão that the main theory was now that Madeleine had died in an accident within the apartment and that all leads on the kidnapping scenario had been exhausted.

This was a bold announcement that the investigating officers were satisfied of the McCanns' guilt and involvement in Madeleine's death and were abandoning any further search for the child. It was also an indictment on the procedures that would halt the search for Madeleine McCann, with the only proof of foul play based on already flawed evidence, eventually to be proved even less trustworthy by a British court trying the suspect in a Real IRA bombing that occurred long ago in a province of Northern Ireland.

CHAPTER 16

Lightning Strikes

Long-time residents of the Algarve would recall that, in the autumn of 1990, similar shockwaves had been felt throughout the community with the disappearance of nine-year-old Rachel Charles.

Rachel disappeared after getting off the school bus of the Vilamoura International School near the home in Vale Navio, Albufeira, that she shared with her mother and stepfather Ray Charles. Instead of going directly to her home, she headed towards a nearby stables, where she had an after-school riding lesson planned.

Witnesses would report a red car with British number plates stopping near Rachel as she walked towards the riding centre. Apparently familiar with the driver, the nine-year-old got into the car and was never seen alive again. During a huge search and rescue operation involving local residents, her body was found four days later in a shallow grave of earth and leaves on Falésia beach, between Albufeira and Vilamoura. She had been strangled but there was no sign of a sexual assault.

Shortly after the discovery, Michael Cook, a young motor mechanic who had worked for Ray Church, Rachel's stepfather, and was known to her family, was convicted of the murder and sentenced to nineteen years' imprisonment. But the case didn't end there. Such was the rumour and controversy surrounding the investigation and the criticism of the police handling of the crime scene and interrogation of Michael Cook that questions were asked in the Westminster House of Commons in 1992 by Dr Robert Spink, member for Castle Point and the unfortunate Michael Cook's MP.

The relevant excerpt from Hansard can be found in the Appendices of this book, but at this point it is only necessary to point out that Cook, who was just five feet tall, white and very obviously English, was presented in an identification parade of burly, dark-skinned and moustachioed Portuguese policemen where he stood out like a black cat in a negative. It was at that point he was identified by a witness, who had failed to recognise him when he was individually pointed out by investigators on the previous day.

Dr Spink also told the assembled MPs that Cook had been brutally tortured to extract a confession, at one point being hung out of the police station's upper storey by his heels, and that 'Cook's lawyers were said to be pushing for the release of a television video report which allegedly showed police beating Cook.' Later, those lawyers were involved in a 'tragic accident' involving a front-tyre blow-out, which incidentally it is claimed has never been properly investigated by the police. In that untimely accident, Dr da Silva was killed and Dr Coelho severely injured.

Other evidence submitted by the prosecution was found to be false. Claims that Cook was a known child molester were untrue and forensic evidence that tyre tracks found near the body were from Cook's car were found to be false. Nonetheless, in a rush to judgment that must have brought a thankful sigh of relief from the Portuguese tourist board, Cook was found guilty and imprisoned. If his conviction was as unstable as Dr Spink MP would have us think, then the truth is that a sexual predator – the judge in his trial was adamant the motive for Rachel Charles's death was sexual gratification despite the lack of evidence of sexual assault – is still at large, not more than 50 kilometres from Praia da Luz.

Even more disturbing are the parallels that the investigation of the McCann case has to that of missing eight-year-old Joana Cipriano, who disappeared from the village of Figuiera near Portimão, 15 kilometres from Praia da Luz, on 12 September 2004. As with the case of Madeleine McCann, the first supposition of the police was that the child had wandered off into the surrounding countryside and found herself lost. Leonor Cipriano began a public campaign with TV interviews and the distribution of posters in an attempt to find her daughter. Meanwhile, suspicion of an abduction followed and a few possible leads were investigated without firm results. The investigating officers' suspicions then turned to Leonor.

Leonor Cipriano was reportedly brutally beaten to extract a confession and photographs of her swollen eyes and battered face published in Portuguese newspapers. Eventually, after an alleged seventy-two hours of brutal interrogation, she confessed that Joana had returned to the house unexpectedly after an errand to a nearby shop and had seen Leonor and her uncle João, Leonor's brother, making incestuous love. Although she withdrew her confession the next day, the police had extracted from her a story of murdering her daughter and dismembering the corpse before scattering the pieces around the countryside. She was sentenced to twenty years, João to nineteen years. But again Portuguese police on the Algarve were accused of extracting a confession by the use of torture and brutality; serious doubt was cast on the verdict, especially when it surfaced that a person within the family's orbit had banked €50,000 shortly after Joana's disappearance: the cost of an eight-year-old girl child?

Similarities to the more recent McCann inquiry stand out against the murky background: both mothers lost their daughters, both began extensive campaigns, though much more limited for want of funds in the case of Leonor Cipriano. There are even more startling similarities to consider. Five detectives who investigated the case of missing Joana Cipriano were arraigned before a Lisbon court accused of misconduct surrounding the extraction of Leonor Cipriano's confession. One of them was DCI Gonçalo Amaral, joint head of the investigation into the disappearance of Madeleine McCann and chief architect of the case against Gerry and Kate McCann as being responsible for their daughter's death.

Amaral was accused of covering for the detectives who physically tortured the confession out of Leonor Cipriano and later relieved of the charges. He was not accused of taking part in the beatings and was the only officer among the accused who belongs to the Faro Judicial Police. All the others worked out of Lisbon.

Apart from the most worrying aspect of the aftermath of the botched Cipriano investigation – that another predator of young girls was probably still abroad in the area– is that one wonders at the possible fate of Gerry and Kate McCann, had they not been British subjects under the constant scrutiny of the UK press? No further arrests have ever been made in the Cipriano case.

While both the McCanns and Robert Murat are left with some quite pertinent questions to be answered by their interrogators, the police must have been aware that two cases involving the abduction of young girls in the area for sexual motives have never been resolved or satisfactorily resolved by an arrest, and that, in the case of Joana Cipriano, the confirmed banking of a large sum of money by a family associate so soon after the child's disappearance does leave open the possibility that, without the mother's knowledge, the child was abducted and sold into the white slave market so prevalent in nearby North Africa. The Portuguese police, especially DCI Amaral, would never admit that possibility but, if that were possible, could Madeleine McCann also have met with the same fate?

CHAPTER 17

Flight of the Imagination

He drove the car into the small parking area off Dr Agostinho da Silva fronting Block 5 of the Montes de Sol urbanisation, the apartments rented by clients of Ocean Club's Waterside Garden holiday complex, parking on the left-hand side in front of the end window of apartment 5A, where he knew his target for this night's work slept unattended.

He had watched for five nights now, after becoming aware of the child's parents' nightly forays to the poolside tapas bar of the complex. He had attracted no attention as he watched from his car that he parked each night opposite the walkway entrance at the rear of the building. At almost regular half-hourly intervals that became less exact as the evenings wore on, he had watched either the Scots doctor or his tall male colleague mount the rear patio stairs and go into the apartment. The reflected shine of streetlights on the patio-door glass originally told him the door shutter wasn't down and the easy entrance of the two men on their rounds told him the sliding door must be unlocked. He knew there would be no outside locking system on the patio doors.

Now he left his car unlocked with the keys in the ignition in case he needed an even faster getaway than intended and walked out of the car park, turned right down Dr Francisco Gentil Martins and crossed to the other pavement to better observe the rear patio of 5A. As he came level with the security gate at the side of the Ocean Club reception building, he saw the Scots doctor emerge from the exit and walk up the hill towards the walkway: the time was 9.06pm.

He sank his neck into the collar of his jacket and turned his head away but the doctor – it was the girl's father whom he'd heard called Gerry by other members of the party – didn't look in his direction. He continued down the hill to turn at the bottom and walk back up slowly as Gerry McCann turned left into the walkway running behind the apartments.

He had almost given up and was deciding to leave his attempt to grab the girl until the next night when the doctor's head appeared above the bushes, walking up the steps to the rear of 5A. The man had chosen to make his move immediately after the usual 9pm monitoring because he had noticed the visits became more erratic as the evening wore on and the child's parents hadn't left their apartment until 8.25pm that evening. But now, with the moment so near, he had a grim sense of foreboding and would have walked back to his car and driven home had he not been aware that the party were due to leave within the next few days. Tonight had seemed perfect but time was slipping away.

He watched Gerry McCann enter the apartment and he sank back even further into the shadows at the bottom of the street to wait. Within a few minutes the doctor reappeared at the top of the patio steps and moved down, his head finally disappearing behind the hedge that bordered the rear garden. But he did not immediately emerge in the street.

The man quickened his stride and cast a look to his left as he passed the mouth of the walkway, the dim light reflecting off his sweating forehead. His heart almost stopped in his chest as he saw McCann, whom he supposed had taken the more roundabout path back to the bar along the walkway, in conversation with another man.

No traffic was in sight and the pavements were clear as he averted his head and crossed the road, continuing up to the junction to linger until he saw Gerry McCann emerge and walk down the hill towards the security gate. He followed downhill and moved swiftly to the wrought-iron gate of the small garden. He pushed it open, entered and closed the gate behind him, then very slowly and carefully he began to mount the steps. A child-gate lay resting against the wall at the top.

Once on the patio he looked to his left across the blue reflection of the floodlit pool to the tapas bar beyond but only the rolled transparent blinds, curled up thickly against the one-storey roof of the building, could be seen above the bushes and trees lining the inside of the perimeter wall. Faint laughter and a shout of triumph drifted across to him as someone claimed a victory in the Thursday quiz night. He would have to move fast. His watch showed 9.15pm.

Having slid open the patio door, he stepped into the living room and checked the main bedroom to his left. It was empty, as he had expected. He moved on along the corridor to the next room on the left. The door was slightly ajar and he stepped through, taking in the two cots and the single divan bed to his left with the slumbering forms of the children. He tiptoed past and put his hand on the canvas strap that ran down beside the window frame and controlled the shutter. He pulled it towards him, then down and the shutter began to rise, squealing softly against its runners. Madeleine stirred and turned over in her sleep.

Once the shutter was high enough to permit a hasty exit he let the strap slide back into place. He turned to one of the cots, where the invading light seemed to have disturbed one of the twins. The boy murmured softly in his sleep and then turned on to his side, away from the light.

As the man crossed back to the bed between the two cots where Madeleine slept, he heard the hiss of the patio door being opened. He froze, cursing himself under his breath for not having followed the logical procedure of locking the door from inside to give himself a few precious seconds to escape. Someone had entered the apartment and was moving towards the bedroom door...

He moved behind the door, poised to slam it against the intruder before running to the open window, its shutter rolled back into its wall box, and climbing through. He could hear the person outside breathing. His senses heightened by the cold fear of discovery, he could almost smell the man who must be there, for he knew that usually only the men made the visits after dark.

Eventually, whoever stood outside the door turned and walked back across the living room. Soon he heard the patio door once again slide across on its runners and his breath escaped with a soft sigh of relief. Discovery had been so close.

He moved silently out of the bedroom and watched a tall figure, its shadow magnified against the backdrop of the whitewashed perimeter wall by the street lamps, walk back down the hill and enter the pool complex by the security gate. The time was 9.48pm: the intruder had been in the apartment for thirty-five minutes.

Moving swiftly, he worked his way along the small corridor to the front door to turn the lock and check outside. The car stood to his right, a few metres away from the low wall and before the window that ended at the front door. No one moved in the dim shadows of the car park and only a few lights showed from other windows along the block. He returned to the bedroom.

Madeleine lay on her back with her eyes closed. As she slept, her breath made small popping sounds. He gazed down into her face. She was such a beautiful child, a veritable angel. He stooped over her and gathered the blanket and sheets around her small sleeping form. As he lifted her up, she made a small, drowsy whisper of protest that came out half-asleep. He pulled her head closer to his chest and left the bedroom carrying his prize.

His heart was beating fiercely against the small, warm

body he held so carefully against his own. With one hand he opened the boot of his car and laid Madeleine down on the plastic sheet that he had laid across the floor earlier. The child was beginning to waken.

Quickly he closed the boot on her sleepy protests and settled behind the steering wheel, barely able to believe that he had achieved what he had planned over the previous five days and hardly dared hope was possible. He started the car and drove slowly and carefully out of the car park...

The dial of his watch showed 9.55pm.

* * *

No one can possibly speculate with any accuracy what fate lay ahead for three-year-old Madeleine McCann that night. The above scenario is based on what might have occurred, according to the McCanns' version of events. Gerry McCann is adamant the bedroom-window shutter was closed when he checked the children at 9.05pm and he recalls speaking to a passer-by identified as Mr Wilkins, with whom he played tennis earlier that day, as he left the apartment after his visit.

Matthew Oldfield's reconsidered second statement tells of seeing the sleeping younger children's forms by the light of the unshuttered window but not that of Madeleine, indicating the shutter had been rolled up in the forty or so minutes elapsing between his visit and that of Gerry McCann earlier – that's if we are to accept Dr Oldfield's second statement, which appears flawed regarding the position of Madeleine's bed from the door, and, like so many statements taken after time is available to reflect, it changed substantially on a second telling.

It is probably immaterial how Madeleine was abducted, although the act of taking the child from her bed hints of a much darker motive than picking up a lost child in the street. But, once she was taken, the only certain fact is that she was gone. There will always be those who prefer to believe their own conclusions on the disappearance of Madeleine McCann, for where would society be without its conspiracy theorists? Nonetheless, while all theories into the disappearance of Madeleine McCann on that night must be heard until disproved, after the many hours of research I have put into the production of this book I find this explanation the most unlikely of all.

CHAPTER 18

Forensics and
Cuddle Cat

Since the declaration by Portuguese investigators of the McCanns' probable involvement in their daughter's disappearance, public mood towards the couple changed to that of untutored suspicion. British police advised both parents to show no emotion before press cameras because a show of grief might well satisfy an abductor's warped psychological needs. Subsequently, while Kate McCann's face displayed the suppressed grief of desolate loss, probably the best expression she could manage, Gerry McCann often appeared cold and without emotion. It was Gerry whose firm clipped voice spoke for them both; it was he who steered his wife through the now-silent crowds as the couple made their way to Padre Pacheco's Church of Light to pray. And, always, clasped in Kate McCann's hands or clipped to her bag was Cuddle Cat, the soft toy so loved by her missing daughter.

The couple had made an emotional plea to the supposed abductor or kidnapper just four days after Madeleine vanished but few now seemed to recall the original sympathy they felt for the grieving parents when they heard those words spoken by Kate McCann on 7 May 2007:

'Madeleine is a beautiful, bright, sunny and caring little girl. She is so special. Please, please, do not hurt her. Please do not scare her, please let us know where to find Madeleine or put her in a place of safety and tell someone where. We beg you to let Madeleine come home. We need our Madeleine. Sean and Amelie need Madeleine and she needs us. Please give our little girl back. *Por favor, devolva a nossa menina.*'

As previously mentioned, Padre Pacheco, the priest of Praia da Luz's tiny Church of Light, felt so much sympathy for the desolate McCanns that he gave them a set of keys to his church to allow them to enter and pray in private as the couple, both known as committed Catholics, sought to avoid the glare of publicity that tragedy so often brings. On 11 August, just a month before Gerry and Kate McCann were declared official suspects by the Portuguese investigators, the priest conducted a prayer service for Madeleine at his church near the sea at the end of the cobbled promenade of the Avenida dos Pescadores.

The public mood-swing concerning the McCanns was a direct result of leaks to the local press from the Judicial Police HQ in Portimão concerning the results of forensic tests carried out by British police conducting their own missing-person inquiry and at the request of the Portuguese. These 'significant' results led to the couple becoming official police suspects, yet the revelations at that time spoke only of a 'key piece of DNA' found in an 'area where it should not have been'. Based on the statements of British forensic officers to date, who constantly warned of the possible inaccuracy of results due to degraded test samples, this could only have been the spots of blood found in the apartment, which would have meant very little and hardly qualified for a 'significant' result because, in the words of British forensic expert Professor David Barclay, 'We know Madeleine was in the apartment and that three-year-olds play and cut themselves all the time.' But the blood found tested as masculine in gender, a fact not printed by the Portuguese newspapers that broke the story.

Other DNA findings that would appear even more bizarre were the result of a search of the Renault Scenic hired by the McCanns twenty-five days after Madeleine's disappearance in response to constant calls for their attendance by the Judicial Police in Portimão. Examination of the boot of the vehicle returned traces of hair, blood and body fluid that could marginally have come from Madeleine McCann, supposing that her body was stored somewhere for more than three weeks before being recovered and placed in the boot of the car, hardly an operation to be carried out in the heat of an Iberian summer, given the high rate of decomposition to be expected in a country where laws instruct on the interment of a deceased person as soon as time has elapsed for the relevant legal procedures to be carried out. Nonetheless, the Portuguese police were delighted at the news and promptly leaked it to the newspapers even as the British forensic teams advised caution.

It seemed that no one in Portimão or Faro had looked at the possibility of articles of clothing belonging to Madeleine – or even her siblings who would possess similar DNA patterns – being placed in the boot of the car when the McCanns switched accommodation from the apartment to a villa in Praia da Luz and used the car to transport their luggage. Nor could many observers understand why investigators did not seize the vehicle and impound it as crucial evidence. The car continued to be used by the McCanns after the questionable testing and was eventually returned to its manufacturer, Renault, after the McCanns' return to the UK. The silver Renault Scenic, registration 59-DA-27, was last seen on a used-car lot just outside Lisbon.

All this speculation was proving too much for the beleaguered McCanns, gagged as they were by Portugal's antiquated investigation secrecy laws. On 9 September, amid a media circus at Faro airport, they boarded a plane and headed for the UK with Sean and Amelie.

Meanwhile in Portugal, buoyed by the '100 per cent' accuracy of the forensic reports, Gonçalo Amaral passed his crime file to the Public Prosecutor. As in most European countries, the Public Prosecutor in turn would pass the file on to an examining magistrate whose task would be to examine the evidence and decide whether there was a case to answer. This was followed by a request to seize a 'potentially vital document' in the Madeleine case, which proved to be Kate McCann's diary. The judge was also asked for permission to seize and examine Madeleine's Cuddle Cat, which had been within the investigators' orbit for almost four months and had been ignored at the scene of the crime when its strange location went unquestioned by the police in attendance.

Following the requests, which were to be refused by the Portuguese magistrate, quoting lack of evidence to prosecute, a French newspaper published a story stating 'forensic evidence' proved Madeleine died from an overdose of sleeping tablets. The report, which was labelled 'ludicrous' by the now-emerging Team McCann, was refuted by British forensic experts, who said the examples were unlikely to be of sufficient quality. The truth was that the British forensic teams had used a method of DNA testing known as 'low-copy number' DNA analysis.

The technique, which was to lead to the collapse of the Omagh bombing trial in December 2007, allowed investigators to examine tiny samples of evidence often many times smaller than a grain of sand. Scientists were then able to grow the DNA to produce the all-important genetic fingerprint to test fully. Samples taken from the McCanns' hire car were tested at Birmingham's Forensic Science Service Laboratory using the low-copy number technique which the Omagh court found to be flawed.

The case against the McCanns was beginning to crumble until an admission by Kate caused rallying supporters to think again. Mrs McCann's revelation in answer to Portuguese requests for Cuddle Cat, Madeleine's soft toy, was that it had been washed. Observers and investigators alike may well have paused to wonder why something so redolent of Madeleine's scent, a tangible remaining memory of a missing daughter, should have been put through a washing machine.

It defied popular logic and would once more shift the ever-changing scales of public support against the McCanns.

CHAPTER 19

Answers in Cyberspace

In these days of digital tracking and the mysteries of cyberspace, where we can send images and texts around the world at the speed of light, there are, according to the UN, 6 billion mobile phone subscriptions in the world.

Everyone, it seems, has the insistent little mobile that rings or buzzes at the most inopportune moments. So it was with the knowledge of a huge task ahead that Portuguese investigators seized the records of all mobile calls made within the areas of Praia da Luz, neighbouring Burgau and Lagos, which form a region with a population of more than 27,000.

The seizures were ordered by Lisbon import Paulo Rebelo, now heading the inquiry from Portimão, and were seen by observers as a sign that the chief inspector had gone back to good old-fashioned policing methods after the results of forensic evidence revealed no breakthroughs other than those imagined by the departed DCI Amaral.

An examination of the seized records could possibly mean Rebelo was moving towards an acceptance of the abduction theory and seeking a conversation between the intruder and an accomplice. Many people who had used their mobiles within the designated areas between 9.30pm and 10pm on 3 May were visited by detectives and asked to identify the numbers they had called.

Gerry McCann and Russell O'Brien were questioned about a telephone call at 11.40pm on 3 May, which was explained as a check on the progress in the search for Madeleine. Both men estimated the distance from each other at four kilometres, yet cell sites gave an improbable 25 kilometres; improbable because both men were with companions who could vouch for their location throughout that night. Nevertheless, the Portuguese press, never doubting their national technology might be at fault, had a field day.

The telephone technicians were using the triangulation method to pinpoint the location of callers in and around Praia da Luz that night. Anyone who has crossed European borders and heard their mobile phone welcoming him or her to the visited country's cell network will know mobile phones emit a signal to a cell site every time they receive or send a call, or when they are switched on or off.

Those signals are logged by phone masts and, by measuring the strength of the signal to local masts, experts can identify, usually to a few kilometres, where a phone was used. The triangulation method of locating a phone has been used in many prominent murder investigations. UK police tried to locate the whereabouts of Soham victims Holly Wells and Jessica Chapman using the same method but knew only that one of the girls' mobiles was in the Soham area when it was turned off by their murderer Ian Huntley.

Although mobile telephones can be traced to within a few kilometres of their exact location and a record will exist of the calls dialled or received, the only existing technology that allows conversations to be monitored belongs to governments such as the UK's Government Communications Headquarters at Cheltenham, England, where a reference in Arabic to a blonde girl, a German and a ferry from Tarifa was picked up soon after Madeleine McCann was taken from her parents. Calls from a stolen cell phone equipped with a new number are untraceable back to the caller.

Nonetheless, the mobile-telephone trace was a welcome sign that, for all DCI Amaral's bluster, the theory of abduction was being taken seriously by Paulo Rebelo. This was further endorsed by the albeit cumbersome request to UK police to trace all known British paedophiles with connections to Portugal and the Algarve.

It was during the UK operation to trace previously convicted paedophiles that many rearrests were made as detectives examined the contents of hard disks of computers in the homes and offices they visited. Each website containing images of child pornography was meticulously scanned for images of Madeleine McCann but none was found. To the Portuguese police, this must have strengthened their theory that no abduction had taken place and focused the investigation more firmly on the missing child's parents, but it also gave Kate and Gerry McCann hope that their daughter hadn't suffered the cruel fate they feared. But, in that case, where *was* Madeleine McCann, and who had taken her and why?

Again, the researcher has to turn to the USA for reliable statistics on child abduction carried out for the purpose of either sexual abuse or monetary gain. The National Center for Missing and Exploited Children (NCMEC) examined 403 attempted kidnappings by strangers or slight acquaintances reported by police or news media in forty-five states from February 2005 to July 2006. The study was conducted to learn how such attempts are foiled but it did not look at successful abductions.

Six in ten victims fought back and escaped, according to the ongoing study's initial findings. Three in ten ran away before any physical contact could take place and about 10 per cent were saved when a nearby adult intervened.

The NCMEC study is obviously dealing with minors capable of fighting back or running away from danger. Statistically, and given a random choice, sexual predators of children select victims aged between seven and twelve years of age.

The Crimes Against Children Research Center at the University of New Hampshire puts it more succinctly with data analysed for 1999 showing that 115 stereotypical kidnappings were reported – ones in which children were abducted by strangers or barely known acquaintances, taken more than 50 miles, detained overnight or held for ransom. Half were sexually assaulted and 40 per cent were killed.

A much larger number of children, around 58,000, were

taken that year for shorter periods of time, mostly by people they knew but not by relatives. In those cases, nearly half were sexually assaulted; less than one per cent were killed. Nearly two-thirds were girls, mostly teens.

Again the predominance is shown of older victims, whether taken by strangers or slight acquaintances. A predator stalking a three-year-old and her parents for five days with a view to kidnapping the child and spiriting her away for his perverted pleasure is a very unlikely scenario, given the existing statistics of incidence.

CHAPTER 20

The Moroccan Connection

The Kingdom of Morocco is located in North West Africa, bordered by the Mediterranean to the north, the Atlantic Ocean to the west, the desert of the Sahara to the south and Algeria on its south-eastern border. The capital city is Rabat, but by far the most famous city is Casablanca.

With regard to Morocco's involvement in child-trafficking, the US State Department issued the following Trafficking in Persons Report in June 2007:

Morocco is a source country for children trafficked internally for the purposes of domestic servitude and, to a lesser extent, commercial sexual exploitation. Morocco is also a source, transit and destination country for women and men trafficked for commercial sexual exploitation and involuntary servitude. Young

Moroccan girls from rural areas are recruited to work as child maids in cities, but often face conditions of involuntary servitude, including restrictions on movement, non-payment of wages, threats, and physical or sexual abuse. Moroccan boys and girls are exploited in prostitution within the country and are increasingly victims of a growing child sex tourism problem. Moroccan girls and women are trafficked internally and to Saudi Arabia, Qatar, Syria, the U.A.E., Cyprus, and European countries for commercial sexual exploitation.

In addition, men and women from sub-Saharan Africa, India, Bangladesh, Sri Lanka and Pakistan often enter Morocco voluntarily, but illegally, with the assistance of smugglers. Once in Morocco, some women are coerced into commercial sexual exploitation to pay off smuggling debts, while men may be forced into involuntary servitude.

The Government of Morocco fully complies with the minimum standards for the elimination of trafficking. Morocco continues to prosecute child sex trafficking crimes, and in January 2007 it initiated a public awareness campaign to educate Moroccans about the consequences of employing child maids. The Secretary of State for Family, Solidarity, and the Handicapped announced a National Plan of Action for Children for 2006–2015 to protect children from mistreatment, violence, and exploitation by creating child protection units around the country.

With specific regard to trafficking of children, the report continues:

The practice of adoptive servitude, in which urban families employ young rural girls and use them as domestic servants in their homes, was widespread. Credible reports of physical and psychological abuse in such circumstances were widespread. Some orphanages have been charged as complicit in the practice. More often, parents of rural girls contracted their daughters to wealthy urban families and collected the salaries for their work as maids. Adoptive servitude was accepted socially, was unregulated by the Government, and only in recent years began to attract public criticism. The problem remained prevalent, although the National Observatory of Children's Rights has conducted, since 2000, a human rights awareness campaign regarding the plight of child maids.

The legal minimum age of employment was 15 years. The number of children working illegally as domestic servants was high: 45 per cent of household employees were between the ages of 10 and 12 and 26 per cent were under the age of 10, according to a 2001 joint study by the Moroccan League for the Protection of Children and UNICEF. The report denounced the poor treatment a number of the children received, such as being forced to work all day with no breaks. Many children worked either as domestic servants, artisan apprentices, or in some other capacity that kept them from attending school.

A report issued in 2005 also made it clear that trafficking of women and minors for prostitution was rife and that prostitution was a problem, particularly in cities with a large number of tourists as well as nearby towns with large military installations.

Prostitution of trafficked minors was a particular problem in the village of El Hajeb near Meknes, as well as in Agadir and Marrakech, which attracted sex tourists from Europe and the Arab Gulf states. To combat the situation the government amended the penal code in 2003 to make sex tourism a crime, while other amendments increased the penalties for promoting child pornography and child prostitution and for employing underage children.

The world does not appear to have changed that much from the late nineteenth century when William Stead, a campaigning British journalist and editor of the *Pall Mall Gazette*, paid £5 for Eliza Armstrong, the thirteen-year-old daughter of a chimney sweep, to illustrate how easy it was in London to procure young girls for prostitution. However, the scheme backfired.

Having embarrassed William Gladstone's government with an account of his investigations in the *Gazette*, entitled 'Maiden Tribute of Modern Babylon', Stead and five others were charged with illegally kidnapping a minor and committed for trial at the Old Bailey. The virtuous and well-meaning Stead was found guilty and sentenced to three months in London's Holloway Prison, then catering for male as well as female prisoners. As a result of the publicity engendered by the Armstrong case, two years later Parliament passed the

Criminal Law Amendment Act that raised the age of consent in Britain from thirteen to sixteen and strengthened existing legislation against prostitution.

Portugal as a nation has a long, dark history in the slave trade at least equal to that of Britain. Barely 10 kilometres from the communities where Madeleine McCann and Joana Cipriano disappeared stands Lagos, the old and notorious slave port that gave its name to a West African city in Nigeria.

By 1854 the Portuguese were importing 1,000 or more Africans a year to work as indentured servants to be freed after a period of service, closely related to the 'bondsman indenture' practised in Britain's Australian and American colonies in the eighteenth century. As a point of interest, it was due to intermarriage between freed Africans and Europeans that many Portuguese are of mixed blood and darker than their Spanish counterparts on that country's northern borders, who inherit the taller stature and lighter skin of their Teutonic forebears.

But the inhabitants of northern Morocco's Rif are mainly light-skinned Berbers, a race descended from the pool of Italians, Sicilians, Spaniards and Egyptians rather than Nigerians, Saudi Arabians and Ethiopians. Many children are fair-haired, though the colour tends to deepen to a light chestnut in adulthood.

The Rif is a mainly mountainous region extending from Cape Spartel and Tangier in the west to Ras Kebdana and the Moulouya River in the east, and from the Mediterranean Sea in the north to the river of Ouargha in the south. It was in this area, full as it was of echoes of the old Arabian slave trade, that virtually all sightings of children resembling Madeleine McCann would be reported.

To be fair to Portugal, the ancient smear of slave trader can be equally directed at her more northerly neighbours. Even present-day Britain, with its burgeoning immigration, has attracted a modern-day slave market fuelled by the old Eastern Bloc *mafiya* and North African elements.

With Portugal's proximity to the North African coastline, one of the less unrealistic theories surrounding Madeleine's disappearance is that she was smuggled to North Africa after her abduction was paid for by a wealthy Arab family. This might even fit in with the theory that she wandered from the apartment looking for her parents and was picked up by a passing North African itinerant, who realised her value in the North African slave market as a young blonde northerner. This is possible, but again asks for the vagary of coincidence to be considered.

But, even if, however unlikely, Madeleine McCann had been picked off the street by a paedophile, there is a faint chance that she may still be alive. According to the experts in such matters, and as discussed earlier, regressive paedophiles are attracted to perfect-looking children and this appeal may have meant that Madeleine has been well cared for, fed and clothed, although sadly the occurrence of regular sexual abuse should not be discounted.

In 1997 a convicted paedophile went so far as to kidnap two ten-year-old girls and hold them prisoner in his Eastbourne flat for three days until police rescued them. In addition, Belgian paedophile Marc Dutroux kidnapped a twelve-year-old girl in 1996 and kept her in a cellar for eighty days.

But the media publicity given to the case of Madeleine McCann may equally have brought about her demise. Standard operating procedure in a kidnapping investigation is to do nothing to cause the kidnapper to panic. Details of the progress of the search are never revealed as this may cause a panicked abductor to dispose of his victim should arrest seem imminent, a lesson obviously never learned by Método 3 with Francisco Marco's ludicrous statement that his agents were almost at the door of the house where Madeleine was being held, as we'll see later.

Blame must also be directed at the press of both Portugal and the UK, whose constant and not particularly accurate reports heightened the profile of the case to very dangerous levels, causing an abductor to know that he cannot risk the public appearance of Madeleine McCann in any circumstances, prompting him to dispose of the evidence while he can.

Certainly, the McCanns consistently refused to accept the possibility of anything other than an abduction of Madeleine from her bed. In answer to those who proposed any other possibility, Gerry McCann was adamant: 'The distance is so small, and it was so close it was almost like having dinner in your garden. What we were doing was rigorous with multiple people checking at regular intervals.

'We're absolutely certain [that Madeleine didn't wander]. We double- and triple-checked and have no doubt she was taken.'

As if to support the idea that a little girl could have wandered off to seek her parents, another story was emerging from eyewitnesses who claimed to have seen a dark-haired man of about thirty-five, 5 feet 7 inches tall carrying a child at about the time that Madeleine's disappearance was discovered. Russell O'Brien's partner Jane Tanner would claim she had seen the man at around 9.25pm and others reported sightings in the area in the minutes leading up to 10pm, approximately the time that Kate McCann appears to have found her daughter missing. However, these latter sightings, to be reported much later in the investigation by an Irish family holidaying in Praia da Luz at the time of Madeleine's disappearance, would figuratively remove Robert Murat from suspicion after Irish father Martin Smith from Drogheda in County Louth confirmed the man they saw bore no resemblance other than in height to the expatriate property agent.

The theory that she wandered out of the apartment, together with the uncertainty surrounding the position of the bedroom window, was beginning to look feasible.

As for the Moroccan sightings, many will have been fuelled more by the possibility of a £2.5 million reward than actual sightings of the missing three-year-old. As such, as many observers warned when such a large amount of money was dedicated to a reward, the search would be seriously compromised and the Fund switchboard swamped with opportunist calls. There was no lack of the latter.

A few days after the Portuguese public prosecutor in charge of the case, Cunha de Magalhães e Meneses, ruled that not enough evidence was contained in the police file to warrant further interrogation of the couple, a photograph was published in UK newspapers of a woman in Morocco carrying a small blonde-haired girl child who, depending on the hysteria of the reader, bore a remarkable resemblance to Madeleine. The Spanish police were said to be taking the sighting seriously.

The thought of a small blonde white girl child in the hands of supposedly black barbarians kept the national dailies in the UK occupied with hysteria for a week until someone pointed out that there is a large number of little blonde girls in northern, once know as Spanish, Morocco since, the Berbers who inhabit the region are predominantly European in appearance, thanks to the long occupation of Spain and its mercenaries – or perhaps we should point the finger at the Crusaders.

The likelihood of Madeleine being smuggled aboard a boat and then taken southward to North Africa, a mere day's sail for a private vessel, was fuelled by the departure of a locally owned yacht on the morning of 4 May, the day following Madeleine's disappearance, and the subsequent failure in attempts to contact its owner, plus a report from the eternally sensible GCHQ at Cheltenham, England, of a telephone transmission intercept – GCHQ Cheltenham listens in to all our satellite phone transmissions – of messages in Arabic referring to the 'little blonde girl', a German man and a ferry from Tarifa, the port on Punto Marroquí in Spain. Added to these possibilities was a disturbing report from Isabel González, a Spanish tourist in Morocco, who told police that on 15 June she saw a girl fitting Madeleine's description being dragged across a street in Zaio by a North African woman. This appeared to link up with the GCHQ report of the telephone intercept occurring on 4 June.

Another report had Madeleine seen with a woman in the village of Fnideq in August. The latter sighting was reported by Naoual Malhi, a Spanish woman of Moroccan origin, and was the most promising to date. According to Sra Malhi, she saw a child who she claims fitted Madeleine McCann's description perfectly, right down to the defect in her right eye. This was an iris coloboma, consisting of a split in the iris from the pupil to the edge of the iris. The child was about to enter a taxi with an elderly Moroccan woman.

It is common practice to share taxis in Morocco, with as many as five strangers sharing the cab while the driver works out the most profitable route for himself and, as a secondary consideration, the most economic journey for his clients. Sra Malhi told police that when she attempted to enter the cab she was stopped by the Moroccan woman, who refused to share with anyone. It was later revealed by the taxi driver that the woman agreed to pay the equivalent of £180, a vast amount of money in the circumstances, to commandeer the cab for herself and the child alone. The trail ended in the town of Housima.

What was taken for granted in these apparent sightings was that the persons involved got near enough to note the unusual and striking congenital eye defect that stood Madeleine apart from most other children and had already appeared on thousands of 'Missing' posters distributed all over Europe by the Find Madeleine Fund. In Madeleine's case, the coloboma formed a black radial strip from the right pupil to the edge of the white cornea at 7 o'clock or 30 degrees clockwise from the bottom of the iris. Such a defect is usually hereditary, although neither Gerry nor Kate McCann has a similar defect. In the small girl it was an unusual and attractive feature, noticeable to strangers.

Spanish police, however, traced the origin of the UK press photograph and identified the girl as five-year-old Bushra Binhisa. In the photo the child was being carried in traditional Berber style in a blanket strapped to her mother's back. The mother, Hafida, was suitably astonished at all the public interest, which concluded with more photographs of Bushra featuring in UK and Portuguese dailies, this time serving no purpose whatsoever as the youngster posed with her equally surprised elder sister.

At about this time, late September, probably prompted by the GCHQ phone intercept, rumours began to circulate of a large palace in Saudi Arabia, the home of a wealthy sheik connected to the Saudi royal family, where a young English child had been purchased as a play companion for a lonely little princess. Not surprisingly, this fairy tale, worthy of a Disney production team but no less credible in an investigation that was already stretching the imagination, was accepted by romantics as a possible fate for the beautiful little Madeleine, a far better option than that suggested by cold reality and offering a more acceptable closure.

Unfortunately, such rumours and reported sightings – one must remember that these were also coming in from all over the world – had to be investigated by a stretched police force whose local chief had apparently already decided on his own solution.

The Moroccan sightings also seemed to have inspired the imagination of Spanish private detective licence number 769, Francisco Marco Fernández, Director of Services and Quality of the Barcelona-based agency Método 3.

As late as 14 December, Sr Marco was making extraordinary statements to the world's press that not only did his detectives know Madeleine's location but also they were preparing to give the police information that would lead to the arrest of the members of the 'international paedophile ring that were holding her captive' somewhere – Sr Marco hedged his bets at this dramatic point – in either North Africa or the Iberian Peninsula. Método 3 also confidently assured the McCanns that their daughter would be returned to them 'unharmed' – one supposes that, after eight months in the clutches of an international ring of paedophiles, 'unharmed' would be an optimistic forecast even for Sr Marco – by Christmas. Cynics would later excuse Sr Marco's failure to deliver by pointing out that he had omitted to name a year.

Método 3 was founded by managing director María Fernández Lado, who ran the company with the assistance of her brother Fernando Fernández Lado, a Barcelona attorney who acted as company financial director, and her husband, Francisco Marco Puyuelo, the agency's administrative and editorial director, who is an attorney and expert graphologist with a diploma in the latter from Buenos Aires. Francisco Marco Fernández of the optimistic forecasts is the son of

Sra Fernández. The now defunct company's Madrid office was located in the Chamartín district and was run by Antonio Tamarit Febrero, a specialist with a Masters in fraud investigation, who managed investigation company Tamesfor until it merged with Método 3 in 1998. Método 3 itself fell foul of the law in 1995 when a raid of its Barcelona offices by police uncovered handguns, ammunition, listening equipment, cassettes and transcripts of taped phone calls, the latter illegal under Spanish law without a judge's order. Agency founder Sra Fernández Lado was pictured in handcuffs after being arrested as she handed a client a cassette allegedly containing an illegal phone-tapped conversation. She had previously been taped by police in an undercover sting in which she allegedly admitted to ordering illegal phone taps in the past.

Also arrested were her husband, Francisco Marco Puyuelo, her son, Francisco Marco Fernández, her brother, Francisco Gabriel Fernández Lado and an employee named Oscar Trujillo. All were released after forty-eight hours and the agency exonerated when an investigating judge ruling that it was a clear-cut case of police entrapment. Of that there was no doubt because detectives had persuaded a businessman to meet with Sra Fernández Lado posing as a client. Such entrapments are illegal under Spanish law, which does not even permit plain-clothes store detectives as this too might be seen as entrapment, posing an invitation to steal apparently unmonitored goods.

Those following the story might well bear in mind that there is no love lost between Spain's police forces and private detective agencies, which are held in the same contempt as journalists who ask too many questions. Francisco Marco Fernández has since declared that the allegations made against the company in 1995 were provoked by Método 3's own investigation into state corruption, an unwise move in any country. That is possibly true but nonetheless Telefónica employee Sergio Sancelestino was later charged with being involved in illegal phone-tapping and industrial espionage linked to the same investigation.

In October 2007, the agency signed a six-month contract with the Find Madeleine Fund, funded by the couple's multi-millionaire backer Brian Kennedy, a double-glazing tycoon now resident in Praia da Luz, at the not ungenerous sum of £50,000 per month. But while Método 3 was recognised by police in both Barcelona and Madrid as a formidable investigation unit responsible for cracking a number of difficult cases involving insurance fraud and falsification of patents and trademarks, success in the search for Madeleine McCann eluded its investigators. The contract, which seemed to assure the McCann legal team of nothing more than cheerful forecasts by the ever-optimistic Sr Marco, was due to end in March 2008. It was renewed despite forecasts to the contrary by a surprised UK and Portuguese press, when McCann spokesman Clarence Mitchell referred to Francisco Marco's misleading reports as 'water under the bridge'.

But Método 3 was at least fortunate in that its base in Spain allowed it to investigate at a distance from the strict and antiquated Portuguese laws that actually make it a crime, punishable by imprisonment, for anyone other than a police officer to interview witnesses of a crime currently under investigation by the state. The charge is of 'interfering with an investigation'.

I had seen such repressive methods in action on my own beat in Spain, where the law also limits discussion of a case with anyone not connected – the Spanish word is *ajena* – to the investigation. But in Spain an inquisitive crime reporter is simply seen as a nuisance to be either harassed or ignored depending on the investigating officer's whim, while in Portugal the very real possibility of prison threatens.

The result was a closed investigation, with witnesses and *arguidos* Robert Murat and the McCanns barred from talking about the case in public and therefore unable to offer a public defence to whatever the investigators decided to accuse them of. In the sad and tragic case of Madeleine McCann, this has led to a confused investigation, full of underground rumblings and flimsy theories produced over long and often alcoholic lunches, pressed into operation and, despite any moral or legal laws to the contrary, leaked to a press force anxious for any copy to fill the next edition.

It is unlikely that little Madeleine will ever be found while such conditions of investigation exist, which effectively bar contact on the ground between an English-speaking press and a local expatriate community who would, as had often been demonstrated to me in neighbouring Spain, much prefer to speak to a journalist in a bar than to a grim-faced officer through an interpreter, whether it be in Alicante or Portimão.

CHAPTER 21

The Missing Children

The hunt for Madeleine hit the UK, Portuguese and Spanish headlines again on 14 January 2008, when it was revealed that a five-year-old gypsy child named Mariluz Cortés had gone missing under suspicious circumstances in the Andalusian city of Huelva, provincial capital of the Spanish border region that abuts Portugal at Vila Real de San Antonio and a fast 200-kilometre, two-hour drive by the N-125 from Praia da Luz.

Mariluz Cortés disappeared near her home in the rundown *barrio* of Alcalde Diego Sayago, an area known familiarly to its ethnic gypsy inhabitants as El Torrejón, after a particular huge low-rent apartment block built by the city housing department. At around 5pm with two companions she had gone to buy *churros*, deep-fried fingers of doughnut mixture popular in Spain, from a nearby kiosk in Parque Moret, no more than 100 metres from her home. Kiosk owner José

Suarez María recalled his son serving the little girl but was unsure whether she was still accompanied by the older girls when she bought her bag of hot *churros* and ran off towards her home. What is known is that she never arrived.

More than 100 uniformed officers were deployed on the search and teams from the city fire brigade's search and rescue canine division raided bins and local rubbish tips for signs of the child.

Following the McCann example in Praia da Luz, within twenty-four hours, colour posters of Mariluz had been printed and were distributed to bars and cafés and handed to passers-by on the streets.

TV crews congregated outside the humble apartment of the Cortés family and the child's parents made an impassioned plea for the return of their daughter. The weeping mother was seen in a television interview pleading for her daughter's abductor to return the child to her family. Tearful, bespectacled Irena Suarez Fernández told the cameras, 'If you have taken my daughter believing her to be lost, please bring her home. If you need money, we will find it for you. We will sell our cars, our home, whatever, just return her to us, unharmed.'

Mariluz's father, Juan José Cortés Ramírez, added, 'There will be no retaliation from the family. All we want is our daughter returned to us.'

More than 500 locals joined in the street search, most of them ethnic gypsies from the area.

Similarities to the case of Madeleine McCann were likely to be drawn by the media and an unsubstantiated report in the local press claimed Mariluz had been seen on a bus with a gypsy woman who was shouting at the child to be quiet. The Cortés family would later admit to a suspicion that Mariluz had been carried off by a band of Romanian gypsies in retaliation for her family having refused the Romanians permission to set up stalls in a Sunday market they run in El Portil.

From my own experiences in the 1970s when I spent two years working and living among the gypsy populations of Madrid and Aranjuez, I know that in these circumstances child abduction among the clans is not unusual. Gypsies live by the code of *contrarios*, when an imagined slight by one family member might see a vendetta lasting for years. It was therefore quite possible, reading between Irena Suarez's words, that the family was aware who had taken Mariluz and her relatives' search may well have been set to extend over Europe. Sadly, however, a vendetta could be ruled out when the unfortunate child's body was recovered on 7 March 2008 from one of the many estuaries of the River Tinto delta that flow around the city of Huelva. An autopsy revealed that Mariluz Cortés had been suffocated and had suffered pre-mortem injuries to her head and ribs before being immersed in the water. It would seem the Cortés family's suspicions had been unfounded, for, while stealing children is not excluded from the gypsy culture, murders of children, especially of their own race, is practically unheard of.

A report illustrating the volatile nature of the Rom, the universal name for the gypsy nation, arrived on my desk at the same time as the report of the disappearance of Mariluz

Cortés. A sixty-four-year-old motorist, identified in the eccentric Spanish manner as 'Gaspar G', since Spanish police never fully identify a victim or perpetrator to the public, had been shot nine times in his car in the gypsy *barrio* of El Vacie in Seville after accidentally running down a seven-year-old gypsy girl who had run into the path of his vehicle from behind a parked car. Such is the Iberian gypsy code of justice.

However, the case of Madeleine McCann had its own reflection on the case of missing Mariluz Cortés, even if the little gypsy's fate was more likely to lie with a daylight abduction off the street by an opportunistic and unbalanced killer. What is clear is that a lesson had been learned concerning a missing child, at least by Portugal's neighbour Spain, where over 100 police were immediately on the street following a report of the child's disappearance . It seems the world was waking up to the plight of missing children.

On announcing its support for International Missing Children's Day, organised by the European Federation for Missing and Sexually Exploited Children on 25 May 2007, the European Commission freely admitted, 'The problem of missing children is complex and multifaceted. It is today not possible to obtain comprehensive statistics across the European Union regarding missing and sexually exploited children. Data gathering is seldom organised at a national level and the available data are largely difficult to access and little or no details can be obtained'.

To give an indication of the extent of the problem in some European countries, the following statistics were obtained from national sources near the time of the initial investigation:

In Italy, police records show that 1,850 minors went missing in 2005. In Belgium, the number of dossiers reported by the police in 2005 was 1,022. In the UK, police recorded 846 cases of child abductions in 2002/03 while the total number of cases of missing children (runaways for any reason) was estimated at 70,000 annually.

In the United States, the only country in the world to provide current statistics on its missing children, the Office of Juvenile Justice and Delinquency Prevention has released statistics that show throughout the USA a child disappears every 40 seconds, a total of 2,100 a day or 800,000 a year. It also estimates that 500,000 child disappearances a year are never reported to the authorities, making that total nearer to 1,300,000. While the USA's statistics do not reflect on Europe, they serve to illustrate the worldwide dilemma of missing minors.

Many are abducted to be exploited as beggars, a multi-million-euro industry in Britain and on the Continent, where appealing children – if wan and ragged enough – can wring money out of the hardest heart. To give an example, four-year-old Denise Pipitone was abducted in a middle-class sector of Milan on 1 September 2004, to be captured in a video shot begging from passers-by in Vía Ettori Ponti on the corner of Piazza Ohm in the same city on 18 October, just over a month later. Sitting brazenly beside the child was her keeper, a fat Romanian gypsy woman, whose employer had probably paid €3,000 or €4,000 for the child as a 'business' investment.

Interpol supplies the following information with regard to Italy's procedures in dealing with reports of missing children:

In Italy there are Offices specialised in children's issues; nevertheless, cases of missing children are generally dealt with in co-operation with investigative authorities (Squadra Mobile – CID) or directly by the Office or Headquarters of the police forces receiving the relevant report. At central level, cases of missing children are monitored and analysed by an Office within the Central Directorate of Criminal Police responsible, inter alia, for the Italian Internet website to search for missing children (www.bambiniscomparsi.it) or (www.missingkids.it) which became operational on March 15, 2000, in co-operation with the US National Center for Missing and Exploited Children. The above site contains photographs and details useful with a view to tracing children.

According to the procedure usually followed to immediately start searches for a missing child following the relevant report, the Questure (Provincial Police Headquarters), also on the basis of information originating from the other police forces, are requested to enter his/her name both in the file of "persons to be searched for" of the Multi-agency Data Bank, specifying the reason for this entry, and in the Schengen Data Bank.

At the same time, the police authority receiving the report forwards a telegram to local police offices again for search purposes (usually to all Offices or to specific ones if there is sufficient evidence directing investigations to this end); the telegram contains information on the missing person, the probable causes of the event and the measures to be taken. If the missing person is believed to be abroad, foreign law enforcement agencies are informed via Interpol channels. Obviously, the above-mentioned procedure is completed by investigations aiming at ascertaining the causes of each event.

Spain, like Portugal, has its share of missing minors but many of the cases reported around the Mediterranean, with the exception of Morocco and Algeria who do not contribute to Interpol's statistic bank, concern children involved in parental-custody disputes who have been taken abroad by one of the parents, often in defiance of court judgments, and never returned to their rightful custodian or guardian.

The method of Portugal's Iberian neighbour Spain in dealing with cases of missing children is similar to Italy, with specialised units employed in investigating the circumstances of the disappearance. Spain and Portugal each support an itinerant population of gypsies, now swollen by immigration from the Ukraine and Romania, among whom begging is the most dominant profession.

The begging gangs are highly organised, operating under a central controller and making use of a pool of children to work the streets. Younger children up to the age of five or six are sent out with keepers to sit and beg. As they grow older and lose their 'puppy-dog' appeal, they are sent to seek handouts from clients at cafés and bars. These latter situations put the children at great risk from sexual predators and paedophiles but their keepers are never far away – not, sadly, to protect the child's interests but their own.

In Spain it is against the law under the 1995 amendments to the Penal Code to be in charge of a child while begging but the law is not strictly enforced except in areas where the presence of ragged children, mewling infants and the ever-present pleas for alms are likely to have a negative effect on tourism.

At the time of Madeleine's disappearance, police in Portugal's neighbour were looking for as many as 200 missing children across the mainland peninsular and the islands. Among these were fifteen-year-old Amy Fitzpatrick, Juan Pablo Martínez and Jeremi Vargas. Of these, the most recent mystifying case of child abduction occurred in Los Llanos in Las Palmas on 10 March 2007, when seven-year-old Jeremi José Vargas Suarez vanished while playing near his home in Santa Lucía de Tirajana. Unusually for a Gran Canarian, Jeremi had fair chestnut hair; his eyes are large and brown. One moment he was there, playing among his friends, and the next moment it was as if he had vanished into thin air.

Amy Fitzpatrick was a pretty teenager from Dublin who lived with her mother, an older brother and her stepfather on the Riviera del Sol urbanisation in Calahonda, Mijas. She disappeared on 1 January 2008 as she took a shortcut home after spending New Year's Day babysitting with a friend in the nearby Calypso area. Amy carried no money, mobile phone or passport; no sign of Amy or the clothes she was reported to be carrying in a bag have ever been found despite searches by police and canine tracker teams.

Another fifteen-year-old who disappeared from the island of Tenerife in 2007 suffered the fate that all parents fear. The body of Fernanda Fabiola Urzúa was discovered near her home after police arrested twenty-eight-year-old Héctor Fabio Franco. Fabio Franco confessed to murder and rape and led police to the grave of his victim.

The case of ten-year-old Juan Pablo Martínez Gómez is even more bizarre. The youngster was travelling with his parents in a tanker lorry driven by his father in Somosierra, Madrid. An accident occurred and the tanker overturned, killing both adults. Juan Pablo was never seen again, following an eyewitness report that a van carrying an adult male and two females stopped at the scene and drove off with the newly orphaned child. The date was 25 June 1986. If alive, Juan Pablo would have celebrated his thirty-second birthday on 1 January 2008. Nothing has been heard of him since the accident. Had he suffered an injury of which he later died? Was he abused and murdered by the 'Good Samaritans' who rescued him? His case is just another mystery on police files of the missing children of Iberia.

In January 2008, in the town of Telde on the island of Gran Canaria, distressed ten-year-old Sandra Domínguez told her parents of an attempt to drag her into a van after she refused the occupant's lure of five euros to enter the vehicle. Within five hours, police were questioning Marcos Javier Rodríguez Cabrera, a thirty-seven-year-old construction worker, who was later charged with attempted kidnap, illegal possession of a firearm and theft of a vehicle after the child picked him out of an identity parade. A specialist anthropologist was later called in to identify bones found at the arrested man's workplace of a pet cemetery to establish whether they were animal or human remains.

Greece presents the most parallel mystery to that of Madeleine McCann, where the island of Kos held the mystery of the disappearance of toddler Ben Needham. Ben was just twenty-one months old when he disappeared on 24 July 1991 while playing on the doorstep of a farmhouse that was being renovated by his grandparents.

On the day of his disappearance, he had been left in the care of his grandparents while his single mother Kerry went to work at a local hotel. His grandmother told investigators she had only taken her eyes off him for a few minutes when it was discovered he was gone, sometime around 2.30pm. The police extensively questioned the Needhams, holding them as prime suspects, and delayed informing airports and docks of Ben's disappearance or widening the search for the child. A shop assistant gave a statement that he had seen Ben on the evening of his disappearance with an older boy but this lead was not followed up until it was too late to trace the boys mentioned in the sighting.

It was the belief of the Needham family for decades that Ben was kidnapped with the intention to sell him for adoption or that he might have been taken by child traffickers. However, there has been no evidence to support this theory and some observers always considered an accident to be a legitimate alternative scenario. The similarity to the McCanns' case is obvious.

There have been various possible sightings of Ben Needham over the years, especially during the first two years of his disappearance, but the most hopeful was in 1995 when a Greek private detective found a blond boy of about six years old, living among gypsies in a camp near Salonika on the Greek mainland. The boy told the detective he had been given to the gypsies after being abandoned by his biological parents. Police attended the campsite some hours later and took the child into protective custody when the man who claimed to be his guardian failed to produce any paperwork. However, the Needhams were not convinced the boy was Ben and no DNA testing was carried out.

In 2016, twenty-five years after Ben Needham's disappearance, new information came to light, indicating that the little boy was crushed by a digger in use near to where he was playing and that his body was hidden from the searchers by workmen. Following this lead, investigators from South Yorkshire Police returned to the island of Kos. After the excavating team discovered a toy car believed to be Ben's on the site, Detective Inspector Jon Cousins then concluded that it was his "professional belief" that Ben died in an accident, although his remains have not been found and the case officially remains open.

We might do well in such cases to ignore the convenient myths of the old folk song about the 'Raggle, Taggle Gypsies – O'. But in this world of unneighbourly distrust no possible scenario should be completely ignored. Consider the report picked up by the UK national media on 25 January 2008 of police raids on addresses in Slough, Berkshire, to free ten children kept in squalid conditions by gangs of Romanian gypsies, Fagin-like, and taught to steal before being let loose among tourists in London's West End.

There, watched carefully from a distance by their Romanian minder, they would pick pockets and carry out theft by distraction – who could resist a tearful lost eight- or ten-year-old asking for help while an equally young accomplice steals a wallet or handbag? Younger children – one rescued by police in Slough was barely twelve months old – are used in begging operations on the street in the style of little Denise Pipitone in Milan, in 2004.

Police have revealed that gypsy gangs that have flooded across Europe since Romania and Bulgaria joined the European Union on 1 January 2007 upped the crime rate across Europe by 530 per cent, not a little of which accounts for crimes committed by children under the age of criminal responsibility.

Even in the UK the minimum age differs. England, Wales and Northern Ireland limit it to ten years while Scotland settles for eight. Across Europe, Belgium goes for a very liberal eighteen years while the Scandinavians, as represented by Sweden, Denmark, Finland and Norway set the legal age of criminal responsibility as fifteen. Belgium's excuse for letting its youth run riot until nearly into adulthood is that, since the treaty parties to the Rome statute of the International Criminal Court could not agree on a minimal age for criminal responsibility, it chose to resolve the question procedurally and excluded the jurisdiction of the court for persons under eighteen.

In the USA, some states have quite sensibly refused to set a minimum age and instead leave such discretion to the prosecutors to argue or the judge to rule on whether the juvenile before them understood that their actions during the crime were wrong. Sadly, no such option exists for those unfortunate children exported from their homes by parents anxious for the cash that will be sent to them each month while their offspring are taught to steal and beg for their gypsy masters. The children's male minders keep their distance from the operation, collecting the cash or spoils later.

Should the child be picked up by police, there is doubt that the little ones even know where they are taken back to each night and the true criminal goes free.

The cash that goes back to Romania is substantial since families who put up their unproductive young to be smuggled across Europe by the gang-masters expect a fair return for their sacrifice, many expecting never to see their children again. Thus, the £3,000–£4,500 paid for a stray child can still be an economic proposition with no strings attached.

Is it therefore unreasonable to believe that someone involved in begging and following the itinerant gypsy lifestyle didn't see a handsome profit to be made on the lost, pyjama-clad three-year-old he or she chanced upon in the streets of Praia da Luz?

CHAPTER 22

The Casa Pia Conspiracy

In 2002 Portugal was rocked by revelations that a highly placed paedophile ring involving the upper elite of Portuguese society – politicians, diplomats and media celebrities – was being supplied with children from the country's longest-established orphan organisation, the Casa Pia of Lisbon.

The Casa Pia is an old Portuguese institution for homeless and orphaned children founded by Mary I, aka Mary the Pious, hence Pia, and organised by her Superintendent of Police, Pina Manique in 1780, following the vast number of destitute children wandering the streets of the capital following the ravages and social disarray left in the wake of the 1755 Lisbon earthquake that levelled the city and killed an estimated 100,000 people.

Thousands of children have since been raised and

educated at the ten colleges that form the Casa Pia network, including many public personalities. As England refers proudly to its Barnardo's success stories so Portugal boasts of its 'Casapianos'. Today, Casa Pia is Portugal's largest educational complex dedicated to helping socially excluded youngsters who lack parental support.

The ten schools or *colegios* that make up Casa Pia provide education for approximately 4,700 students and provide boarding facilities for children in need. The aim is to provide an environment of moral, religious and spiritual values that has sent out into the world many adolescents who later became well-known public figures in Portuguese society. Thus, it was with horror that in 2002 the world learned that children at a Casa Pia college were being regularly subjected to sexual abuse by predatory paedophiles occupying positions of power in the upper echelons of the government and media and that the abuse had been going on since the 1970s.

A preliminary investigation revealed that orphan children as young as eight years old were taken from their beds at night and offered for sex to wealthy patrons who were some of the leading members of Lisbon society, then driven to their opulent homes in a van by a school caretaker, who was the main procurer for the network.

Before being selected for abuse, the children would be checked for sexually transmitted diseases by a high-society doctor who, the young victims told investigators, always drove a red Ferrari. On arriving at their destinations, the children were plied with alcohol before being repeatedly sexually abused.

According to medical records, examinations of the small victims revealed signs of serious sexual assault, including anal rape. Many of the children were able to identify their abusers from marks on their bodies and by giving details of the homes where the abuse occurred. Many prominent people were arrested, including Portuguese TV presenter Carlos Cruz, former ambassador Jorge Ritto and former Socialist minister Paulo Pedroso. Pedroso was an influential member of the opposition who had held the post of Secretary of State for Labour and Training between 1999 and 2001 and as such had been the minister responsible for the Casa Pia homes. He was suspected of fifteen cases of sexual attacks against minors between 1999 and 2000 but the cases against him were dropped and he was freed after spending four and a half months on remand.

As a result, a media circus engulfed the Portuguese capital, each day bringing more tales of decadency and sexual excesses among the capital's elite. The furore lasted two years, when those alleged to be guilty were arraigned for trial, including sixty-one-year-old Cruz, who was accused of homosexual rape of an adolescent and sexual offences against minors. Along with seven others, Cruz went on trial on 25 November 2004.

Following the high-profile investigations and indictments that began in 2002 relating to the paedophilia operation at Casa Pia, the trial involving eight defendants began on 25 November. The defendants faced charges ranging from procuring and rape to homosexual acts with adolescents and the sexual abuse of minors. There were 13,000 pages of files and 790 witnesses scheduled to testify. Charges were based on accusations by seventeen young people, born between 1984 and 1988, who were between the ages of twelve and sixteen when they were reportedly abused in 1999 and 2000, as well as by twenty-nine youngsters, born between 1983 and 1991, aged eight to sixteen when the abuse allegedly occurred. During the investigation, Judicial Police estimated that more than 100 male children out of 4,600 pupils had been sexually abused. Many of the victims were deaf and dumb mutes.

Cruz, as were others named in court, was alleged to have been a client of the Pina Manique College's driver and gardener Carlos Silvino, known as 'Bibi' to his clients, who had himself been a resident at a Casa Pia home. Silvino was arrested and charged with thirty offences of rape against underage residents and of being one of the organisers of a massive paedophile network that involved many important people.

Tessa Costa Macedo, a former Secretary of State for the Family, revealed that she had known of the paedophile ring when she was a minister in the early 1980s but her information – passed in 1982 to the then incumbent president General Antonio Ramalho Eanes – had not been acted upon. Macedo labelled Silvino 'a procurer of children for well-known people who ranged from diplomats and politicians to people linked with the media'.

She also claimed she had handed police details of how children were transported from the orphanage to the homes of their abusers – Silvino, alias Bibi, would drive them in a school bus after they had been certified clear of any sexually transmitted diseases by a visiting doctor who drove 'a red Ferrari'. She also supplied photographs and statements from some of the victims. Sra Costa Macedo said that many of the photographs were found in the Estoril house of Portuguese diplomat Jorge Ritto. Four children who had gone missing from the orphanage were also discovered at the house, where they had been allegedly imprisoned for several days. After presenting the information to the police, Sra Costa Macedo alleged that she was subjected to a campaign of death threats. Portuguese police later insisted they had no records of any documents provided by Sra Costa Macedo.

Another victim of alleged threats in the Casa Pia affair was Pedro Namora, a former Casa Pia orphan and now a lawyer specialising in children's rights and a campaigner on behalf of Casa Pia victims. It was Namora who exposed the whole Casa Pia scandal after learning from a young victim that prominent paedophiles were still using Casa Pia as a 'supermarket' and of how fellow orphans were being tied to their beds and anally raped.

Pedro Namora, who witnessed such abuses himself as a child, told of watching as friends sank into alcoholism and drugs in an attempt to blot out the experiences of a traumatic childhood at the mercy of the Casa Pia network of paedophiles. Namora too has received death threats and telephoned warnings of the grisly fate awaiting his own children, should he not drop his campaign.

He openly thwarted the government by insisting that Portugal is a paedophile's paradise and the network is enormous and extremely powerful. He claimed, 'There are magistrates, ambassadors, police, politicians – all have procured children from Casa Pia. It is extremely difficult to break this down. These people cover for each other because, if one is arrested, they all are arrested. They don't want anyone to know.' The law regarding criminal prosecutions was quietly relaxed ahead of the trial. Repeat sexual offences against the same child now merit only a single charge and a subsequently lesser sentence.

Jorge Ritto, who was a former ambassador to South Africa, retired in 2002 from his post as Portuguese representative to the United Nations Educational, Scientific and Cultural Organisation in Paris, despite rumours of his sexual preferences. These began to circulate when he was transferred from his position as consul in Stuttgart in 1970 after complaints from German police of an incident with a young boy in a park. Files relating to the case were destroyed by the Attorney General's office in 1993.

Following publication of the paedophile allegations, which had begun when the mother of a boarder alleged to Namora that her son had been sexually abused, Prime Minister Jose Manuel Durao Barroso ordered an immediate investigation. President and Socialist Party leader Jorge Sampaio promised the country that 'The impunity which for decades on end has made this case a shame for us all will finally end... Faced with the horror that so many children, who were entrusted to us to be educated and cared for, were victimised it is necessary to declare at this point that the guilty will be severely punished.'

Unimpressed, a spokeswoman from Portugal's own

Innocence in Danger organisation pointed out that her organisation had been warning of child abuse in Portugal for years but there had been a 'virtual media blackout': 'It is no good President Sampaio and Parliament sounding off about the problem now and appearing to be knights in shining armour,' she continued. 'They, like the police, must have known about the widespread abuse of children in Portuguese institutions for years. They have been warned often enough by charities such as ours but for reasons best known to themselves have remained silent. Their recent acts of breast-beating are outright hypocrisy... Time and time again complaint files are lost, witnesses are seldom interviewed and suspects let off the hook.'

Police also detained Joao Diniz, a high-society doctor, the alleged driver of the red Ferrari. In April, they arrested Manuel Abrantes, a former assistant director of Casa Pia. More controversially, the police arrested Paulo Pedroso, Socialist Party MP and Labour and Training Minister from 1999 to 2001 with responsibility for the Casa Pia homes. Pedroso asked Parliament to lift his parliamentary immunity so that police could question him about fifteen cases of child sexual abuse that allegedly occurred while he was Minister. Pedroso claimed he was the victim of a witch-hunt, declaring, 'I have never participated in any act of paedophilia or any similar act.'

The Socialist Party leader at that time was Eduardo Ferro Rodrigues, a close personal friend of Pedroso. Ferro Rodrigues also offered to undergo police questioning after he learned of four children who said they saw him at locations where sexual abuse was taking place. In the light of there being no physical evidence that Ferro Rodrigues was personally involved, Attorney General José Souto de Moura announced he was not a suspect.

As a result of the police tapping of Pedroso's mobile-phone calls, Luis Valente de Oliveira, then Public Works Minister in the government, was also questioned. Sr Valente de Oliveira resigned in April of the same year citing health reasons. However, as a small victory gained from defeat and a backhanded benefit of the child abuse allegations of the Casa Pia scandal, the Portuguese government used the Casa Pia to have far-reaching results on the rights of society because it gave the authorities the power to justify widespread tapping of phone calls by the police and the detention of suspects for up to twelve months without charge.

Following a court order, Portugal Telecom, the national telephone company, supplied Casa Pia investigators with records of 79,000 calls made from 208 private phones between December 2001 and May 2004, announcing it had supplied the phone numbers only and omitted the subscribers' names. But, according to the Portuguese daily newspaper *24 Horas*, no warrants authorising the phone-taps have ever been found.

There were more than 300 pages of transcripts of tapped calls made by Socialist leaders, including Ferro Rodrigues. Under Portuguese law, the police can now tap anyone's phone if they believe this will help solve a serious crime and provided they have special permission from a judge. The Attorney General at the time said, 'I myself could be tapped, whether or not I was under suspicion, if the conversation would help discover the truth.'

On 3 September 2010, Carlos Cruz, Carlos Silvino, Hugo Marçal, Manuel Abrantes, Ferreira Diniz and Jorge Ritto were convicted and sentenced to up to eighteen years in prison due to crimes occurring in the late 1990s and early 2000s. This was the first time an institutional sex abuse scandal had been taken to court in Portugal.

The case had a special significance for the McCanns and Robert Murat. The scandal of Casa Pia brought to light what international agencies like Interpol have long suspected, that Portugal is a historic haven for paedophiles from all around the world due to the presence of high numbers of poor children forced to sell their frail bodies to survive.

At the time, the Casa Pia investigation also held hope for the McCanns in particular because the detective who led the 2002–03 inquiry was none other than Paulo Rebelo, the chief inspector who replaced DCI Gonçalo Amaral as head of the Madeleine McCann inquiry after Amaral was removed following criticism of the handling of their end of the case by Leicester police.

Portimão police now under Rebelo took a deep breath and considered their depiction by the UK press as a bumbling and inept police force whose members, as one veteran journalist put it in a scathing aside, 'couldn't find their own backsides without a mirror on a stick'. Press reports of long alcohol-fuelled lunches in Carvi, the speciality fish restaurant near the police station, hosted by DCI Amaral, had done nothing to endear the foreign press squad to the investigation team, who continued to pass leaked snippets to the more complacent Portuguese reporters.

Much damage had been done to Portuguese pride but with Amaral consigned to his desk in Faro, the UK press turned their critical eye on the Spanish detective agency Método 3 and Francisco Marco's fallacious reports that Madeleine McCann would be home for Christmas. Those not encouraged by the soon-to-be proven empty promises of Método 3, however, might well have taken heart at the new-broom procedures of Amaral's replacement, Inspector Paulo Rebelo.

Determined to go over every piece of evidence that might have been overlooked in DCI Amaral's ill-considered rush to convict the McCanns, Rebelo brought in his own men from Lisbon. Officers previously working on the case found themselves sidelined while detectives from Lisbon's crack homicide division were brought in to Portimão, along with child-sex specialists from the Casa Pia inquiry.

Working on the abduction by paedophiles theory, Rebelo also conceived and supervised Operation Predator that saw raids on more than seventy suspected paedophiles, whose computers were scanned by a team of computer specialists constantly logged in to illegal paedophile websites searching for an image of Madeleine McCann. Rebelo's new approach to the case was summed up when he told a closed meeting of detectives, 'Some officers have developed a closed-mind mentality about the case and the time has come to challenge those pre-conceptions.'

Meanwhile, DCI Amaral had returned to his office in Faro.

Those who have followed the case of Madeleine McCann and despaired at the direction of the inquiry could now take comfort in the fact that it was finally in the hands of a quiet, competent officer with no pre-formed ideas of the guilt of Amaral's *arguidos*, who could now be relied on to take a step back and view the investigation from a new perspective. At the time of taking over from Amaral, Rebelo was quoted as telling his team that the slate was to be wiped clean and any preconceived ideas regarding suspects should be carefully reviewed.

Casa Pia was a shocking case, but it exposed the weak fabric on which the inquiry into Madeleine McCann's disappearance was built and gave fresh hope that the investigation was now in unbiased hands. Now perhaps the search for Madeleine would focus outside apartment 5A and precious police time previously lost in attempts to prove the guilt of the McCanns would be redirected towards finding the victim alive, should that prove possible.

CHAPTER 23

Seismic Shifts

A new law regarding *arguido* status that came too late for the McCanns or Robert Murat was added to Portugal's Penal Code on 15 September 2007, possibly prompted into legislation by the confusion surrounding the definition highlighted in the world's media.

From 15 September, a new procedure was introduced that made it necessary for there to be firm evidence rather than mere suspicion against a person before the status of *arguido* could be applied. The McCanns' Portuguese lawyer, Carlos Pinto Abreu, was moved to admit that he was unsure whether the status would have applied to the McCanns – and Robert Murat – in light of the new code. Certainly no firm evidence as such had emerged to implicate either party in Madeleine's disappearance. The McCanns had been made 'official suspects' just eight days before the new legislation entered the statute books. It is entirely possible that investigators, alerted by the public prosecutor in the case, were aware of the impending change in law when applying *arguido* status to the McCanns on 7 September.

Yet it was in this same month that attitudes towards the McCanns, now back in Rothley with their depleted family, underwent a seismic shift, particularly in Portugal. Magazines and newspapers daily published bland statements made 'by unnamed investigating officers' or by that old and well-loved reporters' standby, 'sources close to the investigation', which, as every journalist knows, translates as 'we made it up'. Even given the fertile imagination of the hacks anxious to fulfil their quota of copy, it is undoubtedly true that much of the raw information published in the press concerning the over-hyped finds in the hire car came from leaks within Portimão police station. Public opinion was seen to sway from sympathy to suspicion and the same old questions re-emerged. Why had Madeleine and the twins been left alone? What did Kate McCann mean by *'They've* taken her'? And just what was the significance of blood and body fluids found in the couple's hire car? Why was Padre Pacheco, Kate McCann's confessor, refusing to be interviewed by police and what were the rumours of searches of the parish church?

While it was true that the amiable Padre Pacheco was seen less and less around the village in his attempts to avoid the denizens of the press, Haynes Hubbard, his contemporary of the Anglican Chaplaincy of St Vincent, whose smaller congregation of the Western District used the Church of Our Lady of the Light for worship – church-sharing is a common practice among expatriate communities whose smaller congregations do not merit a church of their own denomination through the scarcity of flock members – was very much at large and quick to speak in defence of the couple, insisting, 'The church is a place of hope, sanctuary, light, a refuge – and it continues to be so. It has no other function in this community and any suggestion otherwise is ridiculous.

'I hope they [the police] do search it; I hope they search it very well and maybe they can find something. There's a little girl out there who just wants to come home.'

It also became obvious that the Madeleine Fund would not allow the money raised to be used to pay for the McCanns' future defence, should they be charged in connection with their daughter's disappearance.

The Fund's trustees had been informed that there would be no legal impediment to using the Fund, which now stood at £1.1 million, for the payment of legal fees, but one of its directors, Esther McVey, announced, 'The Fund's directors realise there is not only a legal answer but recognise too the spirit which underlies the generous donations to Madeleine's Fund. For this reason the Fund's directors have decided not to pay for Gerry and Kate's legal defence costs.' Gerry McCann's sister and brother, who were involved in administering the Fund, did not take part in the directors' vote on the issue.

Undoubtedly the decision of the Fund's directors, while perfectly sound and honourable, did little to rally supporters to the McCann camp. Many people were now even more convinced that Gerry and Kate and the 'tapas seven' knew far more about Madeleine's disappearance than they were telling the police, an opinion decried by Gerry McCann in his diary entry on the website publicising the search for Madeleine, when he wrote: 'Anyone who knows anything about 3 May knows that Kate is completely innocent. We will fight this all the way and we will not stop looking for Madeleine.'

Nonetheless, his words did little to dissuade public opinion that the events of that night were not exactly as recounted by those sharing a table in the tapas bar.

Was the police version of the time of alert correct and, if so, what had happened in that intervening hour and forty minutes that differs from the McCann version of alerting the police?

But all was not lost for the McCanns, who were about to receive an unlikely champion from, of all places, the Press Liaison office of the Judicial Police. On 16 September, Detective Chief Inspector Olegário de Sousa made his dramatic announcement that his request to stand down from the McCann inquiry had been granted and he would no longer be acting as police spokesman in the case. The reasons for him distancing himself from the case have already been made clear elsewhere, but there is no doubt that the action of this honourable police officer did much to allay fears among the public that the guilt for Madeleine's disappearance rested on the shoulders of the McCanns.

Nor, as September wore into November, could anyone fathom why Robert Murat was still under police scrutiny when even the detectives involved in the inquiry openly admitted there was, to date, no credible evidence against the man other than suspicions that his alibi for the evening of 3 May were open to question. Police would also later reveal that a well-meaning friend, fearing Murat was being put in the frame for the abduction, had told police that, at the time of Madeleine's disappearance, Murat was drinking with him at a bar five kilometres outside Praia da Luz. The friend's false testimony to the Judicial Police joined other misplaced good intentions on the road to hell as it served only to make DCI Amaral and his team even more suspicious of Murat's possible involvement in the abduction.

At that time no one was aware that an eyewitness who had already made a statement to the English and Portuguese police would come forward again in January 2008 to clear Murat of the last suspicion against him that he matched the description of a man who had been seen carrying a small child in a street near the McCanns' apartment on the night of 3 May.

Nonetheless, with the McCanns edged out of the limelight with their return to Rothley – an opinion not shared by the village's inhabitants who were suddenly subjected to the weight of the Fourth Estate in full camera-festooned hunting cry – joint chief of the Praia da Luz inquiry Guilhermino da Encarnação switched the focus back on the expatriate property consultant.

Casa Liliana was again searched, this time involving the removal of interior walls. Much speculation followed the discovery of a basement storage area hidden under the floor of Jennifer Murat's living room but no forensic finds were announced. During the search, no restrictions were placed on the movements of the villa's occupants, Murat and his mother, and Jennifer's dogs were allowed to roam freely about the search area. In particular, detectives wanted to know why Murat had hired a car at short notice two days before he was taken in for the first interview in May. His cousin, Sally Everleigh, expressed her frustration at what she felt was banal questioning of an innocent act by her beleaguered cousin: 'There's nothing suspicious about it at all. He hired the car so that he could go to Portimão to help police to translate. He was just trying to be helpful,' she insisted.

The estranged wife of Murat, who had returned home to Norfolk after a brief attempt by the couple to make a new life with their daughter Sofia in Praia da Luz, was on his side. Dawn Murat, who by then lived with her five-year-old daughter in Hockering, Norfolk, believed in her ex-husband's innocence.

'There is no doubt in my mind he is innocent,' she told the assembled reporters. 'He loves children and is the most kind and generous man I have ever met. I feel for him deeply and I am disgusted at what people are saying. Robert isn't capable of hurting anyone. He has been made a scapegoat.'

Robbed of the McCanns by distance, the Portimão investigators continued to put pressure on Murat. A senior officer, explaining Murat's presence among the police in the early stages of the hunt, said that the expatriate suspect had 'offered himself as an interpreter'. Suspicions formed later meant they didn't use him to translate important interviews. What they had decided was that their most important priority was to find something to link Murat to the missing child and so the unfocused investigation continued, with the spotlight switching between the parents of Madeleine McCann and Robert Murat but failing to remain fixed in any one direction.

Madeleine, meanwhile, had now been missing for almost seven months.

CHAPTER 24

Christmas
in Rothley

While in Praia da Luz the McCann circus, deprived of its star performers, was packing up its marquee, in Rothley plans were being made for a new public appeal for news of Madeleine. Praia da Luz was pulling down 'Madeleine' posters from bars and street posts. Even Padre Pacheco had emerged from the shadows to order the removal of posters from his church, but in Rothley the war memorial was still covered with the symbolic yellow ribbons and many people wore the distinctive yellow wristbands that carry the number of the UK helpline.

On 3 November 2007, the day that marked six months since Madeleine had gone missing, Kate McCann made a special appeal through the news services that was touching in its poignancy: 'Six months is such a long time for a little girl to be separated from her family. We believe that our

Madeleine is out there somewhere and retain hope that we can be reunited.

'Madeleine is a beautiful little person who deserves a loving and happy life. There is no doubt that the best place for her to be, to ensure this, is with her family. We know that somebody, somewhere, can make this happen. *That* somebody has the ability and power to bring about so much joy, as well as bring peace to themselves.'

Praia da Luz residents whom I contacted during that time told me they were heartily tired of the McCann saga while expressing their prayers for Madeleine's safety. I sensed anger in the community that had originally been a willing backdrop for the tragic story but now it was plain that enough was enough. Without doubt, the general consensus was that the story had damaged the community and trade – that ever-present litmus of public opinion – had suffered drastically.

As well as launching the Madeleine Christmas Appeal, there were plans for the McCanns to return to a life bordering on some sort of normality. On 1 November, two days before the six-month anniversary of the tragedy, Gerry McCann returned to his work as a consultant cardiologist at Glenfield Hospital. It had been agreed that, for a couple of months, his duties would not involve physical contact with patients. In truth, some had said they would feel uncomfortable being treated by Madeleine's father.

It was a woeful indicator of the change in public perception of the couple that had once enjoyed the sympathy of parents worldwide. The high-profile public campaign to find Madeleine had become a media circus. Whether they liked it or not, Gerry and Kate McCann had become macabre celebrities.

Back in Portimão, an examining magistrate was already deep into statements given to police by the McCanns and their friends. Inconsistencies were being searched for and the police still hoped desperately for a breakthrough. News from the UK that the McCanns and their holiday dinner companions had reunited for a meeting at a Leicester hotel was greeted with anger by investigators denied the opportunity to re-question the McCanns or their friends by the Portuguese examining magistrate, who felt that the existing evidence did not support a request for further interrogation. His opinion was obviously shared by the Leicester police who, regardless of what international diplomacy might decree, felt that the Portuguese had made a pig's ear of the investigation from Day One.

The failure to secure the site was due to the negligence of the Guarda Nacional Republicana officers first called to the scene. It was their opinion – and they were probably correct – that Madeleine had wandered out of the apartment and that no crime had been committed that led to the failure to secure the site until the arrival of the Judicial Police.

It was down to further negligence by the police that the confusion that reigned that night in apartment 5A was allowed to continue.

CHAPTER 25

Madeleine,
the Movie

News broke on 8 January 2008 that Kate and Gerry McCann had been approached by film company IMG with an offer for a movie deal for the story of their daughter's disappearance. An offer for film rights was rumoured to be £2 million. The news, which hit the front pages of the UK dailies the following day, that representatives of the McCanns had begun negotiations with one of the world's largest entertainment companies came as a shock to the couple's public supporters, who found the idea of a lucrative deal resulting from the tragedy frankly repugnant.

But Team McCann was running into financial grief. The Find Madeleine Fund, which had been launched in May 2007, had raised more than £1.2 million over eight months but donations had dipped to almost nothing after the couple were declared suspects in Portugal in September 2007.

McCann spokesman Clarence Mitchell confirmed that their representatives began talks with IMG in December 2007 but insisted an offer would only be considered if the project was treated 'with sensitivity'. However, plans for a film might have had to take a back seat as the news arrived that Portuguese police were preparing to fly to Britain to sit in on interviews with the couple and their Praia da Luz holiday companions that would be conducted by Leicester police as part of a joint inquiry. Leicester police could only assist in what was developing into an involuntary homicide inquiry at the invitation of the Portuguese police authority while conducting their own missing-person inquiry. The Portuguese were bound by the same territorial laws that barred them from conducting interrogations on UK soil without the collaboration of the McCanns' regional UK police.

Team McCann were probably hoping that a lucrative deal would fund the continuing search for Madeleine amid fears that the £1.2 million that had once filled the coffers from public donations was quickly running out, with the balance standing at only £500,000. Spanish detective agency Método 3 had been paid £300,000 up front by the philanthropic Brian Kennedy for a six-month contract to find Madeleine. Poster campaigns and advertising, although much had been provided free with quarter-page ads in most of the UK dailies, had taken £90,000, and the McCanns' living costs – £4,000 had gone to pay two months' mortgage on their Rothley home, as well as travel costs on commercial airlines despite the generosity of Sir Philip Green of Topshop who occasionally loaned his private jet – had been high.

Media costs had also taken their toll. Spokesman Clarence Mitchell was also being paid by Brian Kennedy – incidentally quelling rumours that he was a government employee installed on the orders of PM Gordon Brown to keep a PR eye on government interests during the months of the inquiry – but the salary of former spokeswoman Justine McGuinness and the costs of a detective agency employed earlier had been met from the Fund.

However, Gerry McCann was quick to deny the story of any film deal. In his blog entry on the official Find Madeleine website, he wrote: 'We can categorically deny that we are considering a movie about Madeleine's disappearance. This is simply untrue. We are approached by a huge number of media outlets regarding a myriad of projects, only a tiny proportion of which we agree to. Each proposal is considered on whether it is likely to have a positive effect, either directly or indirectly, on the search for Madeleine.'

But it was evident that some discussion had taken place earlier, as the blog continued: 'There was a preliminary discussion between a production agency and a representative of Kate and I to discuss the possibility of a documentary about the issues we have faced since Madeleine was abducted. Clearly Europe is a long way behind the USA in terms of its response when a child goes missing.' The last comment of Gerry McCann was probably biased because of the refusal of GNR officers to believe Madeleine had been abducted and their insistence that she had 'probably wandered into the street', albeit the most likely scenario as other more elaborate theories were disproved.

As can be seen from reading the copy of Patricia's Law in the Appendices of this book, legislation calling for immediate response teams in the event of a missing person is only just being considered important enough to be drafted into law in some states of the USA, with the hope of Western missing-person agencies that its influence will eventually spread to Europe.

It is likely that Gerry McCann's statement was written following warnings that the McCanns would risk a public backlash if they were seen to be cashing in on the tragedy of losing their daughter. It is public knowledge among journalists and observers that the McCanns have repeatedly turned down lucrative offers from big-name chat shows and television dramas because of their anxiety to avoid being seen as celebrities.

The directors of the Fund are mostly friends and relatives of the McCanns and they control how the money is used. Although the film deal with IMG appears to have been shelved for fear of adverse public reaction in January 2008, there is no doubt that film and book rights were under constant discussion and review. A film about the McCanns' search for their daughter could use a similar format to that used by IMG in its documentary *Touching the Void*, which recreated the dramatic survival adventure of two British mountaineers in the Peruvian Andes by interviews with the principals and reconstructions of the dramatic high points using actors. But the McCanns must have been aware that such a production could only be filmed if they were exonerated by the police and their *arguido* status removed, bearing in mind that designated suspects in a case, even following the Penal Code amendment of September 2007, are banned from speaking publicly about the events of which they are suspected.

Following the additional news of a proposed book deal, McCann spokesman Clarence Mitchell said, 'We haven't agreed anything; we're not about to sign anything. We like the proposal, we thought it was fair, but there are others to be considered.

'It would be commercially naive if we did not ask for a donation to the Madeleine Fund. We would be giving up the rights to a lot of money that could help to find her.

'Any money raised that way would go to the Fund, which Kate and Gerry do not control. This is not about personal gain for them.

'Madeleine's Fund is spent on investigators and advertising. It's dwindling; the money is going. I would imagine we've got a few months left. It's not going to last the year unless we get more money in.'

Mr Mitchell said a book deal was also being considered 'at some point down the line'. His statement came at the same time as news was released that a Fund director, former *GMTV* presenter Esther McVey, had resigned from the team to concentrate on her bid as a Conservative candidate in a forthcoming election.

To set the record straight, although Gerry and Kate McCann were informed of the writing, content and conclusions of this book through their spokesman and media representative Clarence Mitchell, no request was made either to me or my publisher to contribute to the Find Madeleine Fund. The decisions to do so were made voluntarily and independently during the early discussions of the book.

CHAPTER 26

Return to
Praia da Luz

It was announced in early January 2008 that the Portuguese Judicial Police intended to apply for a three-month extension to the law that normally requires all evidence of an investigation to be made public and those with the status of *arguido* to be formally charged or have the status removed. Although not vigorously enforced in the case of Gerry and Kate McCann, who were allowed to leave Portugal and return home with the twins to Rothley, *arguido* status can impose certain conditions including a ban on travel, the surrender of passports and an order to report to a police station every five days. Equally, in Leicester they were free of harassment from the Portimão investigators who, while under the more benign direction of Paulo Rebelo, still wished to interrogate the McCanns and their companions at length.

A request for questioning to take place with the assistance

of Leicester police in the UK had so far been denied by Home Secretary Jacqui Smith but a return to Portugal would put the McCanns within the Judicial Police's mandate. Meanwhile, the unfortunate group of friends labelled the 'tapas seven' had their own cross to bear. Leaks from witness statements appearing in the Portuguese press claimed some of the group wished to change their stories, casting doubt on the established facts of what took place that night. The leaks also eerily alluded to a possibility that something else happened to Madeleine because much of the investigation in Portugal has focused on what the McCanns' companions allegedly saw that night.

In December 2007, Portimão Judicial Police announced that three detectives were poised to travel to the UK to sit in as British police questioned the Oldfields, the Paynes, Russell O'Brien and Jane Tanner, and Fiona Payne's mother, Dianne Webster. These interviews are believed to have taken place early in 2008 but the McCanns were not required to face questioning put to Leicester police by the visiting detectives. Gerry and Kate McCann planned their return to Praia da Luz sometime after 11 April, when the three-month extension on the investigation had elapsed, with the hope that a stalemate would relaunch the physical search for Madeleine, which has been abandoned by the Portuguese and left to the fumbling advance of Spanish detective agency Método 3, which would solve the case, according to a Spanish police detective of some years' acquaintance, '*cuando las ranas crecen los pelos*' – which translates as 'when frogs grow hairs'.

The McCanns' dilemma was highlighted by their

spokesman Clarence Mitchell when he told the media, 'These unending delays are inhumane. Two parents who have been going through an unimaginable nightmare are being forced to wait another three months. It will be almost a year since their daughter went missing, and even then there could be another extension.'

The whole case, it appeared, had ground to a halt in confusion.

When Madeleine's parents left Portugal on 9 September 2007, they had come to the conclusion that they were being deliberately set up by the police investigating her disappearance. This preoccupation had eased a little with the news that the tenacious DCI Amaral, the detective who had become their arch accuser after the disclosure of the true position of the patio doors, had been removed from the case and sent back to his desk in Faro.

For a brief while, they had hoped that Paulo Rebelo, the ace detective who led the inquiry into the Casa Pia scandal in Lisbon, would look more seriously at the need for a long overdue review of the evidence against them and give some impetus to a renewed search for their daughter but it seemed this was not to be.

Ignoring repeated calls from the couple's lawyers, Rebelo's newly assembled team failed to present tangible evidence against the McCanns and increasingly failed to keep them up to date on the progress of the inquiry. The official cloak of secrecy surrounding the investigation was due to fall on 14 January 2008, but the day came and went with no notice of opened files that would reveal the extent of the

State's evidence against them. Instead came the news of public prosecutor Jose Magalhaes e Menezes's successful application to examining judge Pedro Frias to grant a three-month extension.

Magalhaes e Menezes claimed that the case was 'exceptionally complicated' and required more time. Indeed, it was moving exceptionally slowly. On the principle that everything stops for Christmas in the laidback south, the Judicial Police only commenced preliminary moves for UK interviews of the McCanns and their dinner companions on 7 January, the day after the traditional feast day of the Three Kings, which ends the twelve days of celebration of Christmas in Portugal and neighbouring Spain.

This entailed the submission of all case documents to Eurojust, an EU judicial department set up to allow judicial dialogue between member states. As police enquiries moved ponderously through Interpol in Paris, so the application for interviews would now pass to Brussels for approval before the request was passed to Jacqui Smith at the UK Home Office, who would have to approve the presence of Portuguese detectives during an interview by British detectives on UK soil.

The man advising the 'Gold Group' of Leicestershire police senior detectives in their own investigation of the Madeleine case was Tony Connell, a member of the Crown Prosecution Service's special casework unit. Connell was also in charge of the review that led to the conviction of the killers of Nigerian schoolboy Damilola Taylor, stabbed to death on the North Peckham housing estate on 27 November 2002.

Theoretically, it is possible to prosecute a British citizen for a murder or manslaughter abroad under the Offences Against the Person Act 1861. This was last done in 2005 when Christopher Newman was convicted at the Inner London Crown Court of murdering Georgina Eager in Dublin.

In these days of Brussels bureaucracy, although the possibility of prosecution in a home state exists, it is not possible to cut corners in the pursuit of international interdepartmental co-operation between police forces. Now forms must be stamped and signed before a detective can step aboard a plane and travel to an interview with witnesses – and meanwhile Madeleine McCann is still out there somewhere.

Worse news was to follow near the end of January 2008 when the McCanns read reports that their particular *bête noir* was headed back to Portimão. In an incredible move that could spell disaster for the inquiry, the portly Gonçalo Amaral had been reassigned to the case.

A long-term acquaintance who has worked under DCI Amaral on a number of major crime cases charmingly phrased it for me in a fraught and tense telephone conversation: 'Every criminal in the Faro region fears Gonçalo. He is relentless and never gives up on a case. He never gets credit in the press because he's very unpopular but he's solved a mountain of important cases.'

Despite having revealed nothing about the case, my acquaintance was frantic with worry that his name would be revealed in this book. It won't.

CHAPTER 27

The Stranger

April 20, 2007 was a bleak day in Praia da Luz. The low holiday season was living up to its name with squalls and intermittent rain showers blowing in off the Eastern Atlantic. Green rollers crashed on the shore and seagulls screamed raucously as they wheeled above, hungry eyes wide as they sought their wriggling prey unearthed by the crashing surf.

The man walked in the rain, his long hair wet, his straggling moustache gleaming with droplets of moisture. His thin khaki trousers clung to his legs and he hunched his shoulders against the rain that soaked the collar of the thin combat jacket that his fingers held tightly closed against the squall. His head was down as he kept his eyes on the sand beneath his feet. A man who lived on his wits alone and was ever open to a sudden opportunity, this man was beachcombing for lost coins and valuables.

Gail Cooper, a fifty-year-old holidaymaker, was eating lunch with friends at the Paraiso restaurant that looked out on to the wide curving beach, openly curious at someone who would walk in the rain on a deserted beach. The gaunt stranger strode on, a strange macabre figure alone on a windy rain-swept beach.

She was to see him again later that day, when three hours later, seconds after her husband had left their holiday apartment on an errand, the bell rang. Gail opened the front door to find the bedraggled stranger standing there. He waved a piece of paper at her, as if it were some kind of proof of identity or licence, and told her in broken English that he was collecting for an orphanage in Espiche, a village nearby, where he was helping to care for three children whose parents had died in an accident on the coastal highway.

Such visits are a common occurrence in southern Iberia, where local and expatriate householders regularly deal with itinerants claiming to represent a charity and asking for donations. These people often carry a badly typed document with their photograph attached and offer a small calendar or notebook in exchange for a donation in euros. Often they'll have a story of a sick child and the need for money for an urgent dash to hospital; they all tell a story similar to Gail Cooper's visitor, who offered nothing except his tale of hardship and left after he was rebuffed.

The next encounter would be on 22 April, as Mrs Cooper took advantage of the much-improved weather to lunch with her husband Jonathan at Bar Habana, close to the beach. This time she noticed the man standing near a group of children on a beach outing. She described him as aged thirty-eight to forty-five, with a sallow complexion, lank dark hair, a drooping moustache and large teeth. He had spoken fair but broken English when he begged at her door two days previously.

In the gypsy *barrios* of Madrid, Sevilla and Huelva during the 1970s, I saw such men every waking day. Although the introduction of this new suspect fitted in admirably with my notion of a transient carrying off Madeleine after he'd stumbled across her in the street, I couldn't help thinking the eyewitness's dramatic description lacked only a battered sombrero and crossed *bandaleros* of ammunition to complete the picture of a Mexican villain transposed from the plains of Sonora.

Gail Cooper reported the stranger to police four days after the disappearance of Madeleine McCann and gave a statement at her home two weeks later, but the link wasn't made between the mysterious stranger and the sightings of a man carrying a pyjama-clad child by Jane Tanner and the family of Martin Smith until a UK Sunday newspaper conducted a detailed review of the case, which was read by a member of the McCann team.

The question immediately arose that, if police working under the direction of DCI Amaral from Portimão had considered the theory that Madeleine had wandered from the apartment that night and been carried off by a passing stranger, surely a subsequent call to the public for reports of suspicious itinerants in the community would have started the search for this man sooner? This was obvious from the amount of sightings that flooded the Portuguese switchboard of the McCann detectives in the days following publication of the sketch.

These Iberian wanderers, who are not necessarily ethnic gypsies, belong to a nomadic community of travellers who often live with their family out of poorly maintained old commercial vehicles from which the wife and children set out to beg during the day while the husband searches for scrap metal or a convenient open window and takes to prowling the area at night, looking for any opportunity that may arise to gain a few euros. It is not for nothing that all accessible windows of apartments in Portugal and neighbouring Spain are barred with the inevitable shutters or forged iron *rejas*.

If such a person had come across Madeleine McCann wandering and obviously lost, there is no doubt she would have been picked up and taken back to the wife while a moneymaking scheme was thought out. Whether that would be to sell the child on or return her for reward would depend on the circumstances, but I suspect that, with the furore and activity unleashed in Praia da Luz the following morning, a dirty and battered old commercial van might have been spotted on any highway leading out of town.

I rang a bar in a dusty town in inland Spain, where I knew I would find some of the Spanish gypsies I had known in the past, as ever, sipping their *botellines* of beer and wondering if the sugar-beet factory was hiring for the summer. It seemed they all knew of the case. I put forward my question and heard it passed around. After much thought and extracting a promise that I would pass that way again in the future, they gave me my answer, straight from the horse's mouth. Given the intensity of the McCanns' search for their daughter and the resulting high-profile publicity, a wandering nomad with a fear of the police would be unlikely to approach the family with a view to reward and would be much more inclined to sell her on to an unsuspecting buyer on the road. 'Try the *romanis*,' I was told.

Did they recognise the sketch in the Spanish newspapers? *Coño*, I'd have to call back later since no one had a newspaper, but wait – there was one on the bar. The man looked like a number of possibilities. Without the huge teeth, he might even pass for Eleuterio Sánchez, alias *El Lute*, the famous Spanish gypsy bandit who led the Guardia Civil a merry dance in the 1960s. Perhaps he was a *magrebi* already back in his homeland?

In late spring, the southern ports of Spain are jammed with North African immigrants, *los magrebis*, returning home for the summer. Cars and vans heading for the ports of Málaga and Alicante crowd the *autopistas* south from the French border and east from Portugal, roof racks loaded to precarious heights with furniture, mattresses and blanket-wrapped bundles that seem poised to fall off at every manoeuvre of the vehicle.

It is also bonus time for the busy Customs officials and police, who regularly trawl their nets for luxury cars stolen all over Europe and headed south for resale in the lucrative markets of Saudi Arabia and Bahrain. Did Madeleine McCann leave Europe by this route amid the confusion of what Spanish police describe as *El Gran Regreso* to account for some of the more believable sightings in Morocco?

Throughout this book, I have kept to my own imagined scenario that little Madeleine McCann awoke and took the opportunity offered by the open patio doors to leave the apartment, no doubt in search of her parents. I also believe that she was found and carried off in the way described by Jane Tanner, Martin Smith and his children. What a pity the remorseful parents' first statements read by a stubborn Portuguese investigator and his headstrong deductions should have delayed the search so long.

CHAPTER 28

The Search Goes On

The hunt for Madeleine has been kept alive by the efforts of her parents. Kate and Gerry McCann have literally toured the world in their efforts to keep the search alive and make sure Madeleine remains in the world's consciousness. They have been photographed visiting the Pope in Rome and have appeared on national television in the USA. Their travel and the employment of detective agencies has been financed by the operation of the Madeleine Fund: 'Leaving No Stone Unturned'.

Many sightings have been reported as the world took interest: Madeleine has been reported in South America, Holland, Italy and the States. Many books have been written, including this one. Chief Detective Inspector Gonçalo Amaral tried to justify his theory that Madeleine fell and died in the apartment, even going so far as to cite body fluids discovered in the boot of a car hired by the McCanns some weeks after the child disappeared.

The truth is, nobody knew, but everyone had a theory. When this book was first published in 2008, my publisher made, in my opinion, the mistake of adding a subtitle, or 'screamer' in journalistic slang, which read, 'The Truth About the Disappearance of Madeleine McCann'. I protested to my editor. I didn't know the truth. I could only make an educated guess based on the evidence available. The subtitle stayed and some idiot in the UK defiled me weekly on Amazon until I had to protest. I never knew the truth, but somebody did.

When Madeleine disappeared on the night of 3 May 2007, almost the entire village turned out for the search. Rubbish bins were thrown open and torches lit the wasteland around the village. The child had been taken, but how? Fingerprint experts flooded the apartment, taking samples from the metallic slatted window shutters of the bedroom window. Tests proved that the shutters were impossible to force open from the exterior. A front door had been left ajar but had that been opened absent-mindedly in the search for the little girl? Police tracker dogs found a weak trail leading away from the apartment, finishing 400 metres away outside a closed supermarket, but was it fresh or a remnant of an earlier journey?

The focus turned to the open locking latch of the rear patio door, which had been left open by the McCanns to make it easier to carry out a regular check on the sleeping children. Had the kidnapper entered and left carrying the child that way? If they had, would they have been seen by the vigilant parents from the bar? Had a conversation distracted Kate or Gerry long enough for the kidnapper to leave unseen?

The man whose lot it was to answer these questions was Gonçalo Amaral, DCI at Portimão, asleep in his apartment six miles away. His theories would cost him his job and his pension. He called in the corpse dogs and blamed the parents. A local man, Robert Murat, an Anglo-Portuguese property agent, was also declared an *arguido* and harassed by the press who had taken over the resort. Chief Inspector Amaral was taken off the case in late 2007 and replaced by Chief Inspector Paulo Rebelo from Lisbon, whom Amaral himself replaced a year later.

A young man, absent from the village who had a history of molesting a teenage girl, was declared a likely subject. And still the sightings went on. I thought the child had wandered out of the apartment in search of her parents and been found by the gypsies or itinerants that flooded the Algarve in the holiday season. Children made a good price on the slave market and could be trained as appealing beggars. I gave examples in the text. Like I said, everyone had a theory.

The theories were not kind. People scandalised: in short, either Kate or Gerry McCann, or both, were aware of Madeleine McCann's accidental death and they had hidden the body and, possibly, collaborated with others to mislead police investigators. Meanwhile, the fourth birthday of the missing child came and went – Madeleine would have been four on 12 May 2007 – and the Portuguese police and McCanns continued the search in their different ways.

Portugal had recently suffered the scandal of Casa Pia, a

state orphanage in Lisbon, from which an enterprising and evil caretaker had set up a business hiring the young inmates, many of them as young as six years old, out to wealthy paedophiles for an evening's entertainment. Portuguese tourism reeled under the blow.

Included among those accused were TV personalities and politicians. A predominantly Catholic country could not afford the paedophilic scandal of a young child taken from her bed while the world slept around her. The police were instructed to find the miscreant. Justice would be served and Portugal could breathe again. But it didn't happen.

The Portuguese police reviewed their theories and a flurry of identikits appeared in the press. Some were horrific. Evidently, macabre denizens roamed the Algarve in the early summer of 2007.

Madeleine, meanwhile, had been seen everywhere. She was seen in Germany, Holland, France, Spain, South America and, in a stroke of plundering the well, even in Morocco. The net of the search spread. Madeleine had a blemish in her right eye known as a coloboma. This caused a dark, keyhole-shaped stain on the iris – a condition which is very rare, occurring only in 0.007 per cent of the population. Despite the rarity, the blemish was seen in blonde female children everywhere and duly reported to investigators.

The reports, although well meant, put added pressure on the Portuguese police. CDI Amaral had, meanwhile, concluded his investigation and was convinced that Madeleine had not been taken from the apartment. During the investigation the shutters covering the window of the children's bedroom had proved impossible to open from the exterior.

The British police entered the inquiry at the behest of prime minister David Cameron, sending their own 'corpse dogs' and handlers to Praia da Luz, which caused much excitement when the dogs found traces of body fluids behind a settee in the apartment. The dogs also paid an excited interest in the boot of a Renault hire car that the McCanns had rented twenty-five days after Madeleine's disappearance, provoking speculation on the canines' abilities. Nonetheless, within a few weeks of the dogs' arrival, the Portuguese police seemed intent on proving that the child had died in the apartment and the body removed and hidden for later burial.

The mantle of the perpetrators settled on the shoulders of the grieving parents, Kate and Gerry McCann. On 7 September 2007, the McCanns were declared 'persons of interest' to the investigation. In short, they were suspects in the disappearance of their daughter. Below is a translated extract from the official Policía Judicial intercalary report:

a) The minor Madeleine McCann died in apartment 5A of the Ocean Club in Praia da Luz on the evening/night of 3 May 2007.

b) An abduction was simulated.

c) In order to render the child's death before 10pm impossible, a situation of checking on the McCann couple's children, while they slept, was made up.

d) Kate McCann and Gerald McCann are involved in

the concealment of the cadaver of their daughter Madeleine McCann.

e) At this moment in time, there seem to be no strong indications yet that the child's death was not the result of a tragic accident.

f) From all that has been established up to this moment, everything indicates that the McCann couple, in auto defence, does not want to hand over the cadaver immediately and voluntarily, and that there is a strong possibility that it was moved from its initial location. This situation may raise questions concerning the circumstances under which the child's death occurred.

This damning report on the time of death and the circumstances would result in Amaral leaving the police force to write his own version of events. The police continued their investigation and the McCanns flew back to the UK, where they vowed to continue their search for Madeleine. The Madeleine Fund had some influential and wealthy backers, among them Richard Branson and JK Rowling, and a Madrid-based detective agency was hired.

Within days of the McCanns' arrival in the UK, a photograph taken by a Spanish tourist in Morocco was published amid speculation that the child in the photograph was Madeleine. The child had blonde hair, was the correct age, and the coloboma was evident in the right eye. It was one of the many worldwide sightings that would prove fruitless.

Probably disenchanted by the plethora of false trails which followed the investigation and frustrated by the political pressure both from Westminster and Lisbon to close the case, the investigation faltered and lost impetus and the public lost interest.

The law in Portugal forbids any information of an ongoing inquiry being communicated to the public. Although the rules can be bent in the case of missing children, this was not done in the McCann inquiry, thus the press was committed to making up its imaginary scenarios and stories to sell newssheets, which it did with gusto. The press in Portugal announced the 'off-the-record' titbit from Portimão that the main theory was that Madeleine had died in an accident in the apartment and that all leads on the kidnapping scenario had been exhausted.

Prevented by the Portuguese Public Prosecutor from recalling the McCanns, the Judicial Police succumbed to the political pressure and closed the case. They would not investigate further.

CHAPTER 29

A Global Campaign

The world was agog. Without further investigation the McCanns could not clear their name. A national police body had investigated them and effectively found them guilty. The British press ran riot with stories of political intrigue, and Scotland Yard was besieged with demands to open its own investigation. Portuguese detectives flew to London and met with their British counterparts. The British police were already involved with their contribution of the British corpse dogs, Eddie and Keela.

Meanwhile, the private detective agency hired in Spain by the Find Madeleine Fund and named Método 3 (soon to be lampooned as 'Manolo 3' by the British press) was having startling results. According to its director, Madeleine had been seen in places as diverse as Morocco, Spain, France, Switzerland, Belgium and even Argentina and Guatemala, and would be home by Christmas. Kate and Gerry McCann became celebrities, appearing to tell their story on American TV and meeting the Pope in the Vatican.

In between trips abroad to bring the search to public attention Gerry returned to his work as a consultant cardiologist at Leicester's Glenfield Hospital. The couple had no intention of returning to Portugal to face the questions of the Policía Justicia at Portimão, and by order of the Portuguese Public Prosecutor, the police were forbidden to recall them.

However, throughout September 2007 the Portuguese inquiry continued, but on 19 September the Portuguese Public Prosecutor ruled that there was insufficient evidence against the McCanns, and the director of Portugal's Judicial Police Force admitted that the detectives, pointing the finger firmly at DCI Amaral, may have been 'too hasty' in naming Gerry and Kate McCann as suspects in the disappearance of their daughter.

Although the investigation continued on a low key, the inquiry into the disappearance of Madeleine McCann was effectively discontinued. There were many theories how the three-year-old could have vanished. The unlocked patio door gave a logical explanation of her disappearance especially if she had been picked up in the street by an undesirable, but then, we all know much more now. We know what Amaral wrote, but was it true? And what of the abduction evidence? Had it been fabricated as the police from Portimão suspected? Could the McCanns play out a charade on the night of the 3rd of May and be human? Were they consummate actors or did someone steal into the apartment and kidnap their daughter. One thing's for sure, the press didn't help.

CHAPTER 30

The Leveson Inquiry and News International

The Leveson Inquiry into press reporting standards took place in 2011 after journalists employed by Rupert Murdoch's News International were indicted for phone hacking in 2006. The newspaper cited was the *News of the World*, then under the editorship of Rebekah Brooks, whose journalists were accused of hacking, among others, missing teenager Milly Dowler's mobile phone in 2002. The body of Miss Dowler of Walton-on-Thames in Surrey was later found on Yateley Heath, but the public outcry caused by such flagrant disregard of the rights of privacy of the individual caused the Metropolitan Police to make arrests among the journalist community and for the inquiry to be set up.

Millie Dowler had been murdered five years before Madeleine disappeared, but the case generated general debate over the treatment of victims and witnesses in court after Milly Dowler's family criticised the way they were questioned and cross-examined during the trial of the murderer, Levi Bellfield.

Although the Leveson Inquiry didn't take place until 2011, it came at a time when Gonçalo Amaral's book had been published and his video had promoted the Portuguese police's version of the Madeleine McCann case. Gerry and Kate McCann had lost their appeal against publication of the book and the video and were called to give evidence at the inquiry. There they complained bitterly at their treatment by the Portuguese and British Press. The McCanns gave the most powerful evidence over a two-hour period, telling of the way the press of both countries had treated them since their daughter Madeleine had disappeared in Praia de Luz four years earlier. Kate McCann told the hushed courtroom at the Royal Courts of Justice she had been 'totally violated' by the *News of the World* after its publication of her personal diaries in which she had recorded her thoughts about her missing daughter.

Kate McCann went on to say that the newspaper had showed no respect for her as a grieving mother when it ran the story in September 2008 under the headline 'Kate's Diary: In Her Own Words', a written account of her thoughts at the most desperate time of her life. Gerry McCann asked the court to order an investigation of how Kate's diaries, which were seized and copied by Portuguese police, were leaked to the tabloid. As the McCanns described their life as victims of an overzealous and presumptive press it seemed their evidence was likely to strengthen an argument for a stricter regime of press regulation.

The *News of the World* had been closed by its parent company, News International, shortly after police opened the case against it. The reason quoted was 'lack of advertising' as advertisers hastily withdrew their patronage for fear of being besmirched by association.

Judge Leveson, who was appointed by David Cameron when the Milly Dowling scandal broke, stated the new regulations in 2012, which included a self-governing body of newspaper groups to oversee and censor overzealous reporting methods. The germ of Madeleine McCann's being had helped to change the world of newspaper journalism five long years after she disappeared. Meanwhile, a search of sorts continued.

The Find Madeleine Fund had dispensed with Método 3 and its questionable reports, and employed two ex-Scotland Yard detectives who now laboured in the search for the missing child. Eyewitness sightings continued to come in from all over the world and each one had to be investigated. The hunt for Madeleine, although sidelined, had not been ignored. The search would go on, and in time the Metropolitan Police would enter the fray.

CHAPTER 31

Operation Grange

Under no circumstances can it be said the Met has been a mere onlooker in the search for the lost child. There have been many meetings with detectives in Portugal, and Portuguese police, in spite of the Iberian side of the investigation being put on hold, have both collaborated with and sought advice from the Yard. Leicestershire Constabulary, policing the county in which the McCanns live, has also been following its own enquiries.

Finally, on 12 May 2011, four years after Madeleine's disappearance and on the day that would have been her eighth birthday, New Scotland Yard announced that, at the request of the Home Secretary, it would open its own investigation into the McCann mystery. The work of London's Metropolitan Police Service would take the form of an investigative review of the evidence gathered to date. It was hoped that the police in Portugal would be stirred into reopening its own case. But Lisbon was of the view that no evidence had been found that would warrant the case being reopened but that it would collaborate with the London police inquiry.

It was felt that any progress by the Yard's detectives would force a reopening of the case by the Portuguese. Any funding of the inquiry would be supplied by the Home Office as the case had occurred beyond the Metropolitan Police's jurisdiction. Funding was expected to run into millions of pounds.

The inquiry, known as Operation Grange, was led by DCI Andy Redwood. Redwood retired in December 2014, when DCI Nicola Wall of the Homicide and Major Crime Command took over. Since then, the inquiry team has worked diligently to investigate both the possible guilt of the parents and other theories, including abduction, that have emerged during investigation.

Soon after Scotland Yard opened its own inquiry, Portuguese police announced they would reopen the investigation 'due to new evidence discovered'. On 11 June 2014 Operation Grange requested that the Policía Judicial and the Guarda Nacional Republicana search a horse-shoe shaped piece of land to the west of Praia da Luz. In all, more than 60,000 square metres were searched including drainage ditches, outbuildings and land anomalies that had been noted from the air. Some adjoining areas were also searched. The Portuguese search teams were assisted by teams from the Yard. The deployment, which used ground geophysics and echo-sounding radar equipment, was the largest ever undertaken by UK police in an investigation.

In May 2014, three years after the Scotland Yard inquiry had been launched, Assistant Commissioner Mark Rowley, head of Specialist Crime and Operations, chaired a media update on Operation Grange. Many foreign correspondents attended. No evidence of progress in the case was produced although the media attending the update were assured that the inquiry was constantly investigating new leads in the case. The cost of enquiries to that date totalled £4.7 million.

In April 2016, Sir Bernard Hogan-Howe, head of Scotland Yard, said investigators were currently following one remaining line of inquiry and unless any new evidence emerged, the Metropolitan Police Inquiry would close. He added, 'It's needed for us to carry out an investigation together with the Portuguese and other countries that have been involved. There has been a lot of investigation time spent on this terrible case. There remains a line of inquiry which has to be examined and it's hoped that this will be concluded in the next few months.'

The news of a conclusion was met with disappointment by many holders of theories of just what happened to Madeleine McCann in Praia da Luz ten years ago. If alive, Madeleine would have been celebrating her thirteenth birthday on the twelfth of the month following the announcement. However in March 2017, in news much welcomed by the McCanns, the UK Government provided £85,000 in order to prolong the Operation Grange inquiry for a further six months.

Conclusion

During this in-depth examination of the evidence and circumstances surrounding the disappearance of Madeleine Beth McCann on the night of 3 May 2007, I have studied more than 1,000 pages of reports from observers and eyewitnesses as well as the notes from my own file collected during the first year after she went missing In addition, I have looked at scores of video footage, spoken to journalists, both British and Portuguese, and listened first-hand to some of the Judicial Police detectives involved in the investigation. The limitations imposed by the secrecy law are, I discovered, akin to the road safety speed limit; known to all, but rarely observed. I make no excuses for aiding and abetting such transgressions because a good researcher will take his information from whatever source available. It is then up to him or her how it is interpreted.

As a result of what I saw and heard over the year after Madeleine McCann went missing, I came across no clear indication that a planned abduction took place that night. What I found was a web of deception from the mouths of seemingly responsible witnesses and some uncertainties centred on the so-called 'tapas seven' and even on Gerry and Kate McCann themselves. These were naive digressions from the actual progression of events on 3 May, seemingly told for the most innocent of reasons but they have led to overt distrust and suspicion from the Portuguese police, who knew from the start that the circumstances of the child's disappearance could not be as they were related in the immediate hours following the first alert.

The first thought of the GNR officers arriving at the scene was that Madeleine McCann had left the bedroom she shared with her sibling twins, two-year-old Sean and Amelie, of her own volition to search for her mother and father. It should be remembered that later that night a GNR canine patrol tracked Madeleine's scent to an area 400 metres from her parents' apartment.

It is still unclear whether the patio door was open when the GNR arrived – but if it was, they may have assumed Madeleine herself had managed to drag a chair across to the lock to open it.

It is quite likely that the little girl had a vague notion of where her parents would be because they had taken their children to the pool area on occasions and she probably knew they met their friends there at night.

The very real problem facing the McCanns and possibly

Russell O'Brien and Matthew Oldfield was that the children had been left in *unlocked* apartments, a circumstance likely to bring down on them the wrath of the Portuguese authorities and, as would be seen, the anger and contempt of the public at large. Fortunately, the GNR arriving at the Montes da Luz urbanisation presented the obvious solution to the dilemma – that small children left alone have a tendency to wander. But it was the Judicial Police that would question just how the child had left the apartment if all doors were locked? It was at this point that the enigma of the open/closed shutters appeared.

If an abduction had taken place while the apartment was locked, the abductor must have forced an entry. The rear patio doors in a locked position could not be opened from the outside, so the criminal must have entered through the front window. This possibly explains Kate McCann's statement to police that she had found the shutter *forced* and the window open, but this was where the Portimão investigators about to arrive on the scene would find a problem with the couple's testimony.

As previously explained, the window and patio shutters fitted in apartment blocks 4 and 5 of the Montes da Luz urbanisation, where the McCanns occupied apartment 5A, are manufactured from non-ferrous metal slats linked together to form a continuous sheet housed on a roller in a box set inside and above the window. The roller is controlled by a vertical canvas strap that is set on a ratchet again contained in the room; the security feature of the shutter blind is that it is gravity-fed. Once down and in position, the slats lock into each other and become impossible to break through. Any expat living in Portugal, Spain or Greece who has lost a key knows the problem of trying to gain access to their home through closed shutters.

Any attempt to lift the heavy metal shutters is foiled by gravity. By inserting a bar or jemmy between the window sill and the leading edge of the shutter, the criminal might gain an inch of access by causing a small portion of the shutter to lift on the roller, but, as soon as the lever is removed, the shutter will close down to its original position, leaving obvious tool marks on the leading edge and the window ledge, the latter of which the police noted was covered in undisturbed green lichen.

The Portuguese investigators were now aware that the shutters hadn't been forced, although they accepted the possibility that the sliding window – again impossible to open from the outside without causing obvious damage – might have been left open to ventilate the apartment.

Eventually, the McCanns would be left with no alternative but to own up to the open patio doors as the only possible means of access for an abductor. But the die had been cast. They were now seen as unreliable witnesses with something to hide. Chief Inspector Olegário de Sousa, spokesman for the investigation, would confide in British former Chief Inspector Albert Kirby, the man who led the hunt for the killers of Liverpool toddler Jamie Bulger, that it was obvious neither the window nor its shutter had been tampered with. What could have been a simple admission of negligence and irresponsible childcare in that first instant changed into a situation where the McCanns and their dinner companions had been caught out in a naive transgression that would impede the initial investigation and colour its progress under the cynical DCI Gonçalo Amaral.

Why the McCanns were so convinced that their daughter had been abducted and hadn't wandered from the apartment has never been made clear – perhaps the possibility of an abduction removes the psychological guilt that in the latter case they were solely responsible for her disappearance by allowing her the freedom to wander from their care?

Again, it is easy to see where the Portuguese police were going and without an open door they had good reason. A child was missing from a securely locked apartment; there was no sign that anyone had taken her.

In making a point of that flaw in the McCanns' testimony of that night, their friend Matthew Oldfield's account of events must also be brought into question. Dr Oldfield claimed in a second statement – his first had him standing outside the doors on the patio and listening for sounds of the children – that he had entered the apartment and seen the twins *by the light of the opened shutter*, yet it has been demonstrated that the open-shutter version could only have arisen later, after Madeleine had been found missing. Therefore, it appears that Dr Oldfield was mistaken.

In his second and revised statement to the Portimão investigators, Dr Oldfield is allegedly unsure if the window and shutter were fully open, as they would have to be in preparation for the hasty exit of an adult, yet it would seem obvious that in a darkened room extra light, let alone a strong current of air blowing from an open bedroom window through the apartment to the open patio doors, would have been obvious.

Nor does the doctor admit to seeing Madeleine, although he is sure that he saw twins Sean and Amelie. The reason he gives for not seeing Madeleine is that her bed was hidden from his line of sight but this is difficult to conceive because the door to the bedroom from the hall is hinged on the right. Indignant members of the public went so far as to place a petition on the UK Government's website at 10 Downing Street, calling for the Prime Minister to instruct Leicester Social Services to fulfil its statutory obligation to investigate the circumstances that led to Madeleine and her siblings being left unattended in an unlocked 'ground floor hotel room (sic)'. In response, Leicester County Council insisted it was 'discharging its duties' in a full and professional manner. The petition was rapidly rejected, the reason given being the language it contained. There is no fury like that of an indignant burgher and little thought was given to the concept of 'There but for the grace of God go I', especially not from the McCanns' devil's advocate DCI Amaral, who had already set a manslaughter inquiry on its course.

But eyewitnesses to that night present the possibility of the most logical conclusion of what occurred. Three people would swear in statements that they had seen a man walking south down Dr Francisco Gentil Martins carrying a small child dressed in pink pyjamas, similar to those worn by Madeleine McCann. Jane Tanner, who occupied apartment 5B next to the McCanns, would exit her patio by the steps and look left as she came out of her gate into the cobbled walkway that ran along the rear of the apartment blocks to see a figure carrying what could have been a child. The man, described as dark-haired, between 5 feet 7 and 5 feet 8 inches tall, wearing a dark jacket and beige trousers, was walking south-east, which means he came from the direction of the gate that led down from the McCanns' patio steps into the street.

Martin Smith, from Drogheda in County Louth, was on holiday in Praia Da Luz with his family when they bumped into the man just before 10pm on 3 May. Mr Smith, his son Peter and daughter Aoife were walking north on Dr Francisco Gentil Martins when they saw a man approaching them carrying a small child. In passing the man, Martin Smith made a friendly remark and asked if the child was asleep. He has since told police how he and his family's suspicions were aroused because the man made no response when they asked if the barefoot child was sleeping.

'He just put his head down and averted his eyes, which is very unusual in a tourist town at such a quiet time of the year,' said Mr Smith.

The family had forgotten all about the encounter until Peter Smith tallied the date and time with that of Madeleine's disappearance. The Portuguese police were contacted and the family flew back to Portugal to make a statement in Portimão after speaking with Leicester police. They have had no further contact with the Portuguese investigators.

On 7 May, Gail Cooper, who was holidaying in Praia da Luz in the week before Madeleine's disappearance, would report to the Portuguese police the presence of a seedy-looking stranger in late April, who also fitted the description given by Martin Smith and Jane Tanner. Her statement, one of many alleged to have been deliberately ignored by DCI Amaral because it didn't fit in with his own suspicions, would not appear until nine months later and would spark a huge, but unsuccessful manhunt across Europe and Morocco. However, the detectives who worked on the case from the start in Portimão were quick to defend their early investigation and insisted the original statements of Jane Tanner, Martin Smith's family and Gail Cooper had all been followed up and the suspicious stranger located and eliminated. He was, claimed the investigators, no more than one from the usual bands of itinerants that invade the Algarve and the Spanish Costas during the spring and summer months seeking cash to feed their drug habits.

While that might be so, one wonders why such an early success in the investigation, even if it only involved ruling out a suspect, hadn't been fed to the Portuguese press in the 'leak not speak' strategy employed to put pressure on the McCanns.

But that was to come soon enough, with not just the vague hint of a shadowy figure interrogated and cast loose but an actual name. Late January 2008 saw reporters flocking to the Algarve pig farm of Joaquim Jose Marques, where the surprised owner, admittedly long-haired but sans droopy moustache (easy enough to get rid of) and buck teeth (admittedly more difficult) fought off coach loads of UK and Portuguese reporters with the invitation to couple with one of his hogs. The 'fearsome hunting rifle' with which he threatened the intrepid journalists in photographs taken at 'fearful risk' turned out to be a rusty .117-calibre air rifle. So much for the heroics of the Fourth Estate under fire.

The next unfortunate to be named by the press as the man seen by Gail Cooper was Joaquim Agostinho, a forty-two-year-old cockle picker from Altura, near the Spanish border town of Vila Real de San Antonio, and sometime deliverer of newspapers when cockles were scarce.

Agostinho was much heavier than the 'slim, gaunt figure' described by Mrs Cooper, but he did have long hair, a moustache and two prominent front teeth, which gave him the appearance of a startled Belgian giant when confronted by the newsmen's cameras. Nonetheless, neither the cockle picker nor the pig farmer seemed to be the man sought for Madeleine's abduction and this meant that the search was on again with impetus, this time assisted by the eager eyes of early holidaymakers to the Algarve.

The McCann camp was unconvinced by the Portuguese police's introduction of Marques as a straw dog and vowed the search would go on. Marques, who the intrusive reporters were intrigued to discover, also had a three-year-old daughter with his young English partner – shades of Robert Murat – and Agostinho were obviously not their men.

I feel it unlikely that the man was ever located and identified since the Portuguese would have had to trace and question literally thousands of transients across Iberia and in North Africa rather than light upon an unkempt pig farmer living conveniently locally on a tumbledown hillside farm or a surprised cockle picker from Altura.

The Smiths' description and that of Gail Cooper fitted the

man seen by Jane Tanner nearer to the McCanns' apartment but Martin Smith and his family's statements go further. They are positive the man they saw that night was *not* Robert Murat.

But why would an intruder, who had taken the trouble to stalk the family of a three-year-old – an age not apt to listen to reason when frightened – bother to make an entry into the child's bedroom by stealth and then elect to carry her along a street in full public view? Surely such a careful planner would have had a vehicle waiting in the convenient front car park where he was guaranteed to make his exit?

Thus, the conclusion must be drawn that on the night of 3 May 2007 Madeleine McCann left apartment 5A of her own free will at around 10pm, passing through the open patio doors – forensics, if they had looked, might have found the imprint of small fingers as the little girl pushed the doors open wider to allow herself to pass through – and exited from the bottom of the steps through the wrought-iron gate into the street, where she was approached and picked up by the man seen by the four eyewitnesses.

There was a child gate at the top of the patio stairs but this was not in place for the convenience of those of the McCann party who either listened at or entered through the patio doors to check the children.

What happened after that moment, apart from the sightings by Jane Tanner and Martin Smith and his family of Madeleine being carried away to her fate, is unknown and open only to speculation on behalf of the reader but the possibility of a sexual predator or procurer passing at that inopportune moment in time carries very long odds indeed. More probable is an off-the-street random abduction for profit. This can only be speculation but it is more likely that whoever carried Madeleine off that night was a passing itinerant, who saw her purely as a small child who would bring a handsome profit if sold on in the travelling market of the itinerant gypsies. As an example of the possibility, look no further than the 14 March 2008 edition of southern Spain's *Costa Blanca News*, whose front page carried the report by local reporter Nikki Luxford of two separate attempts within an hour in the coastal resort of Moraira to snatch children of less than two years of age from inside their parents' villas by two women of 'Moroccan or gypsy appearance'. In both cases, waiting outside was a car that sped off when the alarm were raised.

Those of the family of the *Rom*, the descendants of the tribes who moved into Europe from India between 800 and 950 AD and whose Romany language still carries the roots of Hindi tempered by the tongues of the lands its speakers have passed through, have known how to cross borders for generations, but in these days of the Schengen Agreement nothing is simpler than a 50-metre stroll across unmanned checkpoints. The gypsies roam where they will and they take their children with them.

However, stubborn insistence on behalf of the investigators at Portimão that Madeleine died in the apartment, bolstered by claims of forensic reports that would look over-hyped in fiction, allow the investigation only one avenue in which to wander. An admission of the possibility of a street abduction following the acceptance that an abduction from the apartment was unlikely to have occurred would have relaunched the search for Madeleine across Europe instead of leaving the crucial following up of clues to private detectives from the self-promoting Método 3 agency and the optimistic waffling of Francisco Marco. Without a new approach to the inquiry in those early months following the little girl's disappearance, such a possibility didn't exist. Many fear that the mystery will never be solved and the perpetrators of the crime and subsequent cover up will never be brought to justice. So much talk and investigation may have occupied hours that could have been spent in the search. Many, like Gonçalo Amaral, assume that Madeleine is dead and believe she died in Praia da Luz ten years ago. Alternatively, the waves of publicity following her disappearance may have been her death warrant. We do not know.

May 2017 is the tenth anniversary of her disappearance, of the day she vanished. I believed then on the evidence existing and the accounts told that she had wandered from the apartment and been found by undesirables. I haven't changed my mind and I hope, somewhere, a beautiful young teenager is alive and sometimes puzzled by a dim, dark memory of walking a street looking for someone and meeting a person who promised her peace. I hope that was true, for Madeleine McCann will always live in the memories of those who knew her or followed her story as I did. And if that's the only way she must live, so be it.

Danny Collins
Southern Spain
November 2016

Afterword

It was a sultry day on 25 May 1974 when Howard Klein drove his wife and family into the tree-lined camping ground beside the river, approximately 10 miles north of Moab, Grand County, in the state of Utah. In the couple's campervan were their five-year-old son and three-year-old daughter Jenny. Jenny was an appealing child, with big enquiring eyes and hair combed over the left side of her forehead in a distinctive cowlick.

The campground was in the trees and there was a path through the woods that led to the river. There were several people, both adults and children, out by the river. The campground was full because it was the Memorial Day weekend. Jenny's father Howard had gone back to the camper for something and Jenny, who had celebrated her third birthday just eleven days earlier, was playing in the sand. There was a dogfight and everyone's attention was turned to the dogs. When Jennifer's mother and brother turned around again, Jennifer was gone.

Some of the people in the campground appeared to be transients and were never questioned. One of the questionable vehicles was an old car parked between the Klein camper and the river. The family doesn't remember anyone at the campground being interviewed. Mr and Mrs Klein think that the area was used both for overnight camping and day use.

Jenny Klein was never seen again and her disappearance is a mystery that gripped a nation. In Grand County, Utah, Detective Curt Bremer has worked tirelessly on the case, which has always been open.

If Jenny Klein is alive today, she will celebrate her 46th birthday in May 2017.

* * *

During the final editing stages of this book, I was hoping to hear of a discovery that would bring the parents of Madeleine McCann the relief of closure and answer the question of just what happened on that night of 3 May 2007, but apart from the reported sighting of that mysterious gaunt and still untraced transient in the week before Madeleine disappeared, the legal status quo remains unchanged.

Perhaps someday evidence will come to light that will see this case file finally closed but the question remains unanswered: was Madeleine McCann kidnapped or killed? Or, the most likely, unseen by her parents dining in a restaurant 120 metres away and subject only to cursory checks from their do-it-yourself child monitors, did she simply walk out through that negligently ajar patio door to be spirited away by an opportunistic stranger?

The whole investigation has been dogged by uncertainty and ineptitude from the beginning. The crime scene around and inside apartment 5A was not made secure, with the result that vital forensic evidence that would have made it clear whether or not an intruder entered the apartment was ruined. There was no fingertip search of the surrounding area, which is standard procedure for most European police forces, and no house-to-house enquiries made at a time when memories would be fresh. In fact, some properties were never searched nor their occupiers questioned. That may well be a factor brought about by the circumstance of foreign residents and police, both of whom speak only their native language, but it should have formed a vital part of the investigation with interpreters brought in as required.

The list goes on of 'official secrecy' in tandem with poor investigative police work.

There is also no doubt that the demeanour of these two middle-class Leicestershire professionals has not endeared them to the public at large. He is too in control of their actions, her emotions too controlled, and the publicity given by the European media has angered critics of the importance given to the case of one little girl disappearing in a world where thousands of children are abducted, abused, raped and slaughtered each year.

Despite the seemingly cavalier attitude of the early investigation to find Madeleine, the operation was not without its critics. Brazilian-Portuguese activist Ana Filgueiras was scathing about the Madeleine campaign: 'The deployment of resources to find the missing girl is laudable,' she commented on being told that 800 uniformed officers were deployed on the case, 'but it is regrettable that the same does not happen in the cases of people who are less well-off.

'Across the globe, but especially in Africa, Latin America and Asia, the kidnapping of children is almost routine but the phenomenon receives little coverage from media that are more interested in reporting each and every detail of the disappearance of a British girl even though the case is insignificant in statistical terms.

'In Portugal we have never seen a deployment of this magnitude. When Portuguese children go missing no TV station airs photos of the victims, but in Madeleine's case we are watching a soap opera conceived to boost ratings and readership to a maximum by playing on people's feelings.'

Perhaps Sra Filgueiras might be forgiven her words of censure in light of her courageous work in setting up the Brazilian Centre for the Defence of Children's Rights in the 1970s to draw attention to the killing of street children by military police in Rio de Janeiro.

In Portugal, SOS Criança Desaparacida of the charity Apoio à Crianza investigated 31 new cases in 2006 of missing children. According to UN children's fund UNICEF, 1.2 million children are trafficked around the world every year.

What was painfully clear as the first anniversary of 3 May 2007 came and went is that only a few theories remain to be proven or disproved. There is a possibility that, as her parents dined with their friends, the three-year-old was abducted from her bed by a predatory paedophile who had watched the family for days, then taken to another location and there either sexually assaulted and murdered, or sold on to a paedophile gang for use in the underground sex market.

But given that the McCanns arrived in Praia da Luz only five days before Madeleine's disappearance and the family routines and timetables that would have to be studied and committed to memory to carry out such a bold venture, it seems improbable in a quiet off-season locality like Praia da Luz that no one noticed the constant and ominous presence of a stranger lurking near the family. In any event, abductions and kidnappings of this nature are meticulously planned by experts for many days, weeks and even months. No professional kidnapper or seasoned abductor would attempt such a bold venture after only four or five days of observation. How can one establish a pattern of movements over just a week?

It's true, despite the hysterical denials of the Portuguese tourism board, that the country is known to attract paedophiles, lamentably many of them from Britain. A ring of 20 Britons set up in Portugal in 1990 was filming sex acts with local boys and sending the tapes to Belgium and the Netherlands. Some of the adult participants were later jailed in the UK and the case was a prime mover in a British government decision to make it illegal for Britons to have sex with underage children abroad. Portugal, it should be remembered, is also the scene of the notorious Casa Pia investigation, conducted by Paulo

Rebelo, who took over the Madeleine investigation after the removal of DCI Gonçalo Amaral.

The most probable theory is that she wandered out of the apartment through the unlocked patio door and was found by a passing stranger, who could have submitted her to one of the fates described above but more probably carried her off for eventual sale on the notorious *ruta mendigante*, the beggars' circuit that stretches all over Western Europe.

Despite the constant warnings of stranger-danger given to today's children, the sexual abuse of a minor is usually committed by a family member or a close and trusted family friend. Statistically, a small child has more chance of choking on a peanut than of being snatched from the street by a sexual predator who just happened to be passing at the time.

Nonetheless, if a child is abducted, it is rarely from inside a house by someone not known to the family. Again, statistics prove that most children abducted by strangers are taken off the street in an unguarded moment and during daylight.

Many liberals may see the selection of the third theory as a slur on the transient beggar population but it is an established fact that this industry is in operation all over Europe. This third scenario also brings the fragile hope that Madeleine is alive and being cared for after a fashion.

The idea that she was abducted for sale to a paedophile ring of the magnitude of the Casa Pia conspirators defies the obvious logic that such an organisation would hardly wish to bring publicity on itself by kidnapping a British child on holiday in the tourist-conscious Algarve.

None of the theories in play is likely but all are possible

and, like the equality of men in Mexico, some are more possible than others: the fact remains that one of them must have happened that night. As in the case of little Jenny Klein, it is a mystery that defies comprehension – and like all great mysteries probably has the simplest of answers.

Meanwhile, we must suppose the earlier refusal of the Portuguese authorities to accept abduction, either from the apartment or from the street, as the most likely scenario will see the unlikeliest of suspects, Madeleine's parents and Robert Murat, under suspicion for life with Madeleine portrayed as the sweet Fanny Adams of the twenty-first century.

Meanwhile, there is hope that Madeleine McCann, like other children, who have lived through the trauma of abduction and been found years on, is still alive.

Hope, after all, in the case of Madeleine McCann is all that is left.

Appendices

Extract from Hansard, House of Commons Debates, 9 June 1992

12.23 am

Dr. Robert Spink (Castle Point): *Rachel, a 9-year-old girl, was murdered by strangulation in a car on the Algarve in Portugal in November 1990. Michael Cook, a friend of Rachel's family, was convicted of the murder in February this year and sentenced to 19 years imprisonment. He was tried by three local judges without a jury. The House will hear that the conviction is unsafe.*

I must start with every possible word of sympathy for Rachel and her family. I see that my hon. Friend the Member for Arundel (Sir M. Marshall) is here because of his concern for his constituent, the victim's mother.

There can be no greater evil than such a crime. I would not defend in any way a child murderer, but I will defend my constituent's right to a fair trial. My responsibility and my job tonight is to highlight the possibility that my constituent may be the victim of a gross miscarriage of justice. Some say that Cook is innocent; some say that the police investigation was inadequate. Some say that the trial verdict was so lacking supporting evidence as to be incredible. Some say that Cook has been tortured and mistreated. Those are not questions which the House can or should decide. In truth, I do not know whether Cook is innocent or guilty. What I do know is that many questions are raised by the case which have the most serious implications, not only for Michael Cook, but for all British subjects travelling abroad.

Let us review some of the evidence. There was, understandably, immense local pressure to clear up this horrible crime. An unsolved child murder would frighten away tourists. An elderly Portuguese gardener said that he saw the murderer and the murder car. He said that the car was red with foreign plates. Cook had such a car. It was alleged that Cook's car tyre marks were found where the body was discovered, and on that prime tyre mark evidence Cook was arrested. It was claimed by the police that Cook had a child-molesting record and that he had confessed to the crime: they had their man. The public furore and the subsequent relief at Cook's arrest were surpassed only by the total outrage against him.

Let us examine the initial key facts. After nine months in gaol, Cook got two good lawyers and it was quickly discovered that the prime – indeed the only – hard evidence linking Cook to the murder was bogus. The tyre marks were of an entirely different type from those of Cook's car. It is also claimed that Cook's car does not have the ground clearance needed for the area where Rachel was found. Similarly, no confession was ever presented at the trial. It had been claimed by police that two officers heard the confession. One remembered it clearly; the second denied all recollection of it. One would not expect to forget such a thing easily.

Cook appeared in court, with black eyes and a missing tooth, and he was deeply bruised. It is claimed that Cook was hung from an upstairs window by his feet, that his feet were beaten until he could not stand, that he was tied to a chair and beaten, that he was deprived of sleep, and that a revolver was forced into his mouth and the trigger pulled in a mock execution. Cook's lawyers were said to be pushing for the release of a television video report which allegedly showed police beating Cook. Those lawyers were involved in a tragic accident involving a front tyre blow-out which, incidentally, it is claimed has never been properly investigated by the police. In that untimely accident, Dr. da Silva was killed and Dr. Coelho was severely injured.

What of the final piece of the early evidence – Cook's record as a child molester? It too is quite bogus. At the trial, the police tried to rescue some credibility on the point. An officer said that Cook had been seen abusing a child a few weeks before Rachel's murder. One might wonder why that was not mentioned at the time. Nevertheless, the judge asked the officer how he knew that. The officer replied that someone, unnamed, had told him. The judge accepted that so-called 'evidence' as clear and unequivocal. I must inform the House that I know of no evidence that Cook has ever posed any threat to children.

I do know of evidence suggesting that Cook is safe and trustworthy with children. I am not aware of any conspiracy and I make no allegations. However, it must be said that Cook was a good target to be 'fitted up'. He has a minor criminal record and he was working unregistered on the Algarve in the motor trade. Indeed, he may have hung himself as his initial account to the police of his movements could have been inconsistent because he thought that he was being questioned about a petty crime.

Let me return to the old gardener – there is always an old gardener in such tales. He changed his story at least twice; his memory, it seems, was greatly assisted by the police. The car was indeed red and foreign, he said; but so was Rachel's stepfather's car, and many others in the area. He also saw Cook talking to Rachel. Cook was, he said, wearing sunglasses, although it would have been almost dark at the time.

The gardener had no difficulty, however, in picking out Cook from an identification parade – at least, *not after the police had specifically pointed Cook out to him, asking, 'Is that the man?' Not that that was necessary; Cook was a white, 5ft-tall, slightly built Englishman, while the rest of the parade consisted of burly, dark, Portuguese policemen who were obviously of Mediterranean origin. Hon. Members may be horrified to learn that, much earlier than that parade – indeed, the day after the body was found – Cook was shown to the gardener by the local police, and the gardener said that Cook was not the man whom he had seen on the fateful day in question. He changed his story. Clearly, the police case needed boosting, so the most incredible thing happened: a reconstruction of the crime was forced on Cook.*

The police said that, in the reconstruction, Cook had shown them the exact positions in which they had found Rachel's school bag and shoes. They said that those items had been thrown by Cook from a fast-moving car over many kilometres on a country road down which he can seldom have been before, some weeks after the alleged event. Even the police blushed when they told that one in court.

Let me now review the harrowing scene of the crime. Again, I sincerely apologise to the victim's family, but this has to be done. A pathologist stated that Rachel struggled furiously for her life in the front passenger seat of a car; it took four to eight minutes to kill her by strangulation. Rachel naturally fought hard, and had the blood of her murderer under her fingernails.

No sophisticated DNA or type matching of the samples was ever presented to court. No evidence was ever presented even to show the simple blood group of the murderer. Such basic blood-group evidence could not have proved that Cook was the murderer, but it could most assuredly have proved his innocence. Hon. Members may feel very uncomfortable about the fact that that evidence was lost, and we should ask why it was lost – or, worse, why it was not used. What, then, of the other forensic evidence? We can all imagine the horrific struggle – that frantic four or eight minutes. Surely the car would exhibit many clues; law experts feel that that must be so. Incredibly, however, not a single link was found between Cook's car and Rachel, or her clothes. The Sunday Times *stated: 'Not a single hair, fibre, bloodstain or sign of damage was found in Cook's car. And Police did not find it unusual that Cook had not cleaned the entire car in an effort to erase prints ... When the body was found, no forensic search was made of the area and no tests were carried out on a bloodstain seen under a fingernail. The body was cremated within days and without extensive forensic examination.'*

Therefore, the defence was denied the possibility of conducting the necessary independent tests. Is not that beyond belief?

Let me now turn to the pathologist's evidence, starting with the astonishing point that the report was tampered with. It has lost – for ever, it seems – its important front page, which gave, among other information, the time of death. The pathologist, apparently, is now unavailable.

The Sunday Times *reported: 'Such post mortem work that was done was minimal'.*

However, a pathologist hired by the defence who examined Rachel's organs said that she might have been killed 24 or 30 hours before her body was discovered, which apparently indicates that she may have been held alive by her murderer for up to two days. She was discovered four days after she disappeared. Cook was first in police hands the day after she disappeared.

That brings us to the alibi evidence and suggests that Cook had the best possible alibi – he was in very close contact with or in the custody of the police, but the judges dismissed that, the pathologist's evidence. Moreover, there was the condition of Rachel and her clothes when found. They were clean and dry. That is consistent with the defence pathologist's findings. The weather had been dry the day Rachel was found, but the previous days had been wet, thus suggesting that Rachel had been dumped only the day she was found.

That evidence was also disallowed by the judges. They chose, as they can under Portuguese law, to refuse to hear some evidence. In a trivial case, that may have been justified, but, in the circumstances, hon. Members may feel that that was an extraordinary piece of selectivity. What is even more remarkable, though, is that the person who found Rachel's body was never called to give evidence, and therefore his evidence was denied to the defence.

Additional alibi evidence comes from Cook's workmates, who saw him a maximum of 10 minutes after he was said to be seen by the man on the horse at the place of the body. The times were precise and checked, but the distance of the two sightings put them a minimum of 12 minutes apart, with no allowance for any other activity at all. That would have been impossible to achieve. That evidence was also rejected. According to the pathologist, Rachel was strangled with a nylon rope. A nylon rope, a jumper matching the one Rachel was wearing and a blanket which was covered with pine needles, as was Rachel's body, were all seen in a car, but not Cook's car. They were seen in Rachel's stepfather's red foreign car. The police did not investigate or use that evidence.

The stepfather certainly had a violent nature at times. Rachel's mother was said by a neighbour sometimes to flee to her home for sanctuary with the neighbour and to stay there with her overnight out of fear of her stepfather's violence. Several people say that they saw scratch marks on the side of the stepfather's face and his arm the day after Rachel disappeared. Some have pointed a finger at the stepfather, but the House cannot and must not assume anything – that would be quite wrong. In a further twist, the stepfather died tragically precisely one year to the day after Rachel was killed, the third death in this story. Therefore, his confession *cannot be tested. I raise those points not to incriminate in any way Rachel's stepfather but only to illustrate, as is my clear duty, the late evening shadow of doubt which is cast over the conviction of my constituent.*

I now refer briefly to the trial and verdict. We have seen that there was no jury and that the three judges were local. They were inexperienced in trying such an unusual case. In Portugal, judges are able to dictate entirely what evidence they will admit and what they will refuse even to hear. With so much evidence lost, destroyed or refused by the judges, Cook's trial was fatally flawed.

The basis of the judges' verdict was made clear in their summing-up. There was a total lack of hard forensic evidence, but sadly there was no lack of hearsay. For instance, members of the Portuguese Institute of Fingerprints told the court the judges said 'with conviction', that Cook's way of life and his friendship with Rachel's family indicated that he was the murderer. Sadly, those fingerprints experts produced no fingerprint evidence.

The judges implied that no motive whatsoever was found, and Cook was not accused of any particular motive. There was no sexual interference of any kind with Rachel. In Portuguese law, first-degree murder requires a motive and premeditation, I understand. They seemed curiously absent. The judges said nothing of substance that I can find in the translation of their summary, except that, as Cook knew the family, he must

261

be the murderer. I turn, briefly, to the appeal. The hearing may not take place until June 1993. That delay would be intolerable. The appeal cannot question the evidence produced at the trial. That evidence, such as it is, with all its flaws, is considered to be irrefutable. For instance, the police evidence that Cook was a child molester cannot be questioned. Yet we know that it should be.

In the appeal lawyers may question only the admissibility of the evidence under Portuguese law. That raises yet a further grave misgiving because incredibly Cook and his lawyers are not allowed to attend the appeal. Those in the House who believe that justice should be seen to be done may be staggered by that revelation. As my predecessor Sir Bernard Braine wrote: 'There is little likelihood that even by the Appeal justice will be done'.

Presumably the matter can be argued in the European Court later. Meanwhile, I have three objectives for the debate. First, I wish to bring pressure on the Portuguese authorities about the possible miscarriage of justice and to allow the earliest possible appeal consistent with a fair and safe hearing. Secondly, I wish to prevent any torture or mistreatment of Cook and to signal to all nations that human rights must be upheld. Thirdly, I wish to thank the Foreign Office for its help and advice so far, which has been professional and appropriate – no blame can lie with it – and I ask the Minister to provide a monthly written report from the British consular staff on Cook's physical and mental condition. In addition to those three *things, I seek a general review of the help which consular staff give to British citizens arrested abroad.*

In summary, there are substantial grounds to believe that a miscarriage of justice may have occurred. First, the conduct of the police investigation is in question. Secondly, the conduct of the trial and the basis of the verdict are in question. Thirdly, I place full trust in the Portuguese justice system to ensure that the appeal is fair. Fourthly, there are grounds to question the physical and mental treatment of Cook. Fifthly, the European Court and the European human rights body may eventually need to intervene if the appeal cannot answer the many questions raised. But I trust that that will not be necessary.

I understand that Cook is considering starting a hunger strike. That would hamper my efforts and I most strongly urge him not to do so, particularly in his poor physical condition. We are told that he is prematurely grey. His bodyweight is down to seven stones. He is skeletal. He has three ulcers. His remaining teeth are rotted. He is withdrawn and paranoid. As a child murderer he has suffered many attacks in prison. He bears two knife scars and many burns scars to prove it. He is alone in a foreign gaol, unable to speak the language. He needs our help. But I stress again that we cannot judge the case from our position here.

I sincerely thank the Minister for his advice and support so far, which is also much appreciated by the family. All British citizens must know that, when their back is against the wall and all seems lost and they feel that the world has deserted them, there is a place – this honourable House – where their basic human rights will be upheld and that there are men and women who will fight for their rights, including their right to a fair trial. My fight does not end here tonight. Here, indeed, it begins.

12.43 am

The Parliamentary Under-Secretary of State for Foreign and Commonwealth Affairs (Mr. Mark Lennox-Boyd): *The House will be grateful to my hon. Friend the Member for Castle Point (Dr. Spink) for bringing this important case to its attention. I note the presence of my hon. Friend the Member for Arundel (Sir M. Marshall), who represents his constituent, the mother of Rachel Charles. I should like to outline the action taken by Her Majesty's Government on behalf of Michael Cook and his family since his arrest. On 5 December 1990 the British consulate in Portimão was informed that Michael Cook had been arrested the previous day for the murder of Rachel Charles. The consulate was told that he had confessed and would be taken before a judge on 6 December to be formally charged. The Portimão consul visited him on 6 December. On that occasion he said that he was being well treated and had no complaints. A Portuguese police officer was present throughout that meeting.*

On 10 December the Portimão consul had a private meeting with Michael Cook. On that occasion Mr. Cook said that he had been beaten twice: once when detained for questioning on 22 November and subsequently after his arrest on 4 December. He said that he had confessed under duress. He claimed to have been beaten on the chest and feet; this, he said, explained why there were no signs of ill treatment.

On the following day, at the consul's insistence, Michael Cook was asked by the prison staff whether he wished to see a doctor so that a formal complaint about his mistreatment could be made. He declined to do so. Also on 11 December the British consul in Lisbon told Mr. Cook's Portuguese lawyer that the embassy would make a formal complaint if Mr. Cook wished. The offer was not taken up either by the lawyer or by Mr. Cook during subsequent visits by the Portimão consul. Thus, no medical examination to substantiate the allegations or otherwise took place.

From 11 December 1990 to 30 January 1992 when his trial began, Michael Cook was visited seven more times by consular officials. He complained once, in February 1991, of having been threatened verbally by other inmates, but said that the threats had ceased. Twice he complained of suffering from mental stress and three times from ulcer problems. The British consul on those occasions sought and received assurances from the prison governor that Mr. Cook would receive the necessary treatment.

The consuls from Lisbon and Portimão attended the first day of Michael Cook's trial, and the Portimão consul attended the last day, 7 February 1992.

On 19 February Michael Cook's brother, Colin Cook, rang the embassy in Lisbon to say that he had heard that

Michael Cook had been stabbed in prison in Faro. The embassy immediately made inquiries. It was assured that Michael Cook had not been stabbed, although he had been involved in an argument over cigarettes with another prisoner. The following day the vice-consul from Lisbon visited Mr. Cook. Although physically all right, he was understandably extremely upset over the trial verdict. The prison governor gave assurances for Mr. Cook's safety. On 4 March 1992, Michael Cook was transferred to Coimbra high security prison, about 110 miles north of Lisbon. During that month, the consul and vice-consul drew the attention of officials at the Portuguese Ministry of Foreign Affairs to the great degree of British ministerial, official and public concern about Michael Cook's case. On 8 March The Sunday Times *published an article reporting that Mr. Cook had been ill treated at the hands of other prisoners. The pro-consul in Lisbon looked into those allegations without delay. He contacted the prison governor on 10 March to register the embassy's concern for Michael Cook's safety and welfare. He was assured that there was no evidence of ill-treatment. Later that day, the vice-consul spoke to Mr. Cook by telephone. Mr. Cook said that one inmate – not a cellmate – had uttered a verbal threat, but that he had not been physically attacked. He mentioned that he was suffering from a stomach ulcer and had dental problems. In response to this, the vice-consul said that the embassy would write to the prison governor about these problems. A letter was sent on 13*

March. On 6 April Coimbra prison confirmed to the embassy that Michael Cook had been given a full-time job in the prison car paint workshop. It also confirmed that he had seen a doctor about his ulcer and had been put on a special diet. He had also seen a dentist.

On 16 April, the consul visited Michael Cook for two hours in a private room. Mr. Cook confirmed that he had gained some weight as a result of his special diet, and did not wish to have any matter raised with the prison authorities.

Michael Cook recently told his parents that he had been taken to see a psychiatrist. He was under the impression that the prison was trying to have him committed to a mental home, which would make it even more difficult for him to prove his innocence. Coimbra prison has told the consul that Michael Cook did not in fact see a psychiatrist. He was taken to see a specialist about his stomach ulcer. Unfortunately, it appears that the prison mistakenly translated 'specialist' for 'psychiatrist' when talking to Mr. Cook. The consul will visit Mr. Cook again on 19 June.

I have described the full support given by the consuls in Portimão and Lisbon. Prisoners Abroad, an admirable organisation run by our former colleague in the House, Keith Best, has been in regular contact with Michael Cook and is giving him full support. I know that Michael Cook, his family and others believe that there has been a miscarriage of justice. I can well understand their concern, but, whatever we may think, it would be wrong for me to express an opinion on the conduct of the trial while an appeal is pending. If the lawyers believe that the case has not been dealt with in accordance with Portuguese law, it is their responsibility to take appropriate steps. Portuguese law provides for this and, indeed, the lawyers have submitted an appeal on Michael Cook's behalf. They have told the British embassy that the Portuguese supreme court has accepted the appeal and that, in their view, the appeal process is proceeding satisfactorily.

On 19 February Colin Cook complained to the British consul in Lisbon that the trial violated article 6 of the European convention on the protection of human rights and fundamental freedoms. On examination, he agreed that the European convention can be brought into play only when all local remedies have been exhausted. We are keeping in close touch with Mr. Cook's lawyers and the Portuguese authorities. We are asking them to do what they can to ensure that Michael Cook's appeal is heard by the supreme court with the minimum delay. Our ambassador in Lisbon wrote to the Portuguese Ministry of Foreign Affairs on 3 June to press this point, and I will be in touch with my hon. Friend as soon as I have a reply.

I fully appreciate my hon. Friend's concern about this case, but I hope that he will understand from what I have said that we cannot intervene until the Portuguese legal process has taken its course. Until then we shall, through our consular officials, continue to visit Mr. Cook regularly and to offer him and his family all the support that we properly can. I shall continue to keep my hon. Friend fully informed.

Appendix 2

Draft of Patricia's Law concerning new legislation on missing persons
(Sponsorship Updated As Of: 5/18/2007)
ASSEMBLY, No. 3643
STATE OF NEW JERSEY
212th LEGISLATURE
INTRODUCED NOVEMBER 9, 2006
Sponsored by:
Assemblywoman VALERIE VAINIERI HUTTLE
District 37 (Bergen)Assemblyman GORDON M. JOHNSON
District 37 (Bergen)
Assemblywoman JOAN M. VOSS
District 38 (Bergen)
Assemblywoman LINDA R. GREENSTEIN
District 14 (Mercer and Middlesex)

Co-Sponsored by:
Assemblyman Steele
SYNOPSIS
'Patricia's Law;' model Missing Persons Legislation.
CURRENT VERSION OF TEXT
As introduced.
A3643 VAINIERI HUTTLE, JOHNSON

AN ACT concerning missing persons, designating the act as 'Patricia's Law,' and supplementing Title 52 of the Revised Statutes.
BE IT ENACTED *by the Senate and General Assembly of the State of New Jersey:*

1. As used in this act:
'Law enforcement agency' means a department, division, bureau, commission, board or other authority of the State or of any political subdivision thereof which employs law enforcement officers.
'Law enforcement officer' means a person whose public duties include the power to act as an officer for the detection, apprehension, arrest and conviction of offenders against the laws of this State.

2. A law enforcement agency shall accept without delay any report of a missing person.
No law enforcement agency may refuse to accept a missing person report on the basis that:
a. The missing person is an adult;

b. The circumstances do not indicate foul play;

c. The person has been missing for a short period of time;

d. The person has been missing a long period of time;

e. There is no indication that the missing person was in the jurisdiction served by the law enforcement agency at the time of the disappearance;

f. The circumstances suggest that the disappearance may be voluntary;

g. The person reporting does not have personal knowledge of the facts;

h. The reporting individual cannot provide all of the information requested by the law enforcement agency;

i. The reporting person lacks a familial or other relationship with the missing person; or

j. For any other reason, except in cases where the law enforcement agency has direct knowledge that the person is, in fact, not missing and the exact whereabouts and welfare of the subject individual are known to the agency at the time the report is being made.

3. At the time of a missing person report is filed, the law enforcement agency shall seek to ascertain and record the following information about the missing person:

a. The name of the missing person, including any aliases;

b. Date of birth;

c. Identifying marks, such as birthmarks, moles, tattoos and scars;

d. Height and weight;

e. Gender;

f. Race;

g. Current hair color and true or natural hair color;

h. Eye color;

i. Prosthetics, surgical implants, or cosmetic implants;

j. Physical anomalies;

k. Blood type, if known;

l. Any medications the missing person is taking or needs to take;

m. Driver's license number, if known;

n. Social security number, if known;

o. A recent photograph of the missing person, if available;

p. A description of the clothing the missing person was believed to be wearing at the time of disappearance;

q. A description of notable items that the missing person may be carrying and wearing;

r. Information on the missing person's electronic communications devices, such as a cell phone number or email addresses;

s. The reasons why the reporting person believes that the person is missing;

t. Name and location of missing person's school or employer, if known;

u. Name and location of missing person's dentist and primary care physician, if known;

v. Any circumstances that may indicate that the disappearance was not voluntary;

w. Any circumstances that indicate that the missing person may be at risk of injury or death;

x. A description of the possible means of transportation of

the missing person, such as the make, model, color, license, and VIN of a motor vehicle;

y. Any identifying information about a known or possible abductor or the person last seen with the missing person including:

(1) name;

(2) a physical description;

(3) date of birth;

(4) identifying marks;

(5) the description of possible means of transportation, such as the make, model, color, license, and VIN of a motor vehicle; and

(6) known associates;

z. Any other information that can aid in location the missing person; and

aa. Date of last contact.

4. a. The law enforcement agency shall notify the person making the report, a family member, or any other person in a position to assist the law enforcement agency in its efforts to locate the missing person by providing to that person or family member:

(1) general information about the handling of the missing person case or about intended efforts in the case to the extent that the law enforcement agency determines that disclosure would not adversely affect its ability to locate or protect the missing person, to apprehend or to prosecute any persons criminally involved in the disappearance;

(2) information advising the person making the report, and

other involved persons that if the missing person remains missing, they contact the law enforcement agency to provide additional information and materials that will aid in locating the missing person, such as any credit or debit cards the missing person has access to, other banking or financial information and any records of cell phone use;

(3) in those cases where DNA samples are requested, the law enforcement agency shall notify the person or family member that all such DNA samples are provided on a voluntary basis and shall be used solely to help locate or identify the missing person and shall not be used for any other purpose;

(4) the law enforcement agency, upon acceptance of a missing person report, shall inform the person filing the report that there are two clearing houses for missing person's information. If the person reported missing is age 17 or under, the person filing the report shall be provided with contact information for the National Center for Missing and Exploited Children. If the person reported missing is age 18 or older, the person filing the report shall be provided with contact information for the National Center for Missing Adults.

b. If the person identified in the missing person report remains missing for 30 days, and the additional information and materials specified below have not been received, the law enforcement agency shall attempt to obtain;

(1) DNA samples from family members and, if possible, from the missing person along with any needed documentation, including any consent forms, required for the use of State or Federal DNA databases;

(2) dental information and x-rays, and an authorization to release dental or skeletal x-rays of the missing person;

(3) any additional photographs of the missing person that may aid the investigation or an identification. The law enforcement agency shall not be required to obtain written authorization before it releases publicly any photograph that would aid in the investigation or identification of the missing person; and

(4) fingerprints.

c. All DNA samples obtained in missing person's cases shall be immediately forwarded to the New Jersey Forensic DNA Laboratory for analysis. The laboratory shall establish procedures for determining how to prioritize analysis of the samples relating to missing persons cases;

d. Information relevant to the Federal Bureau of Investigation's Violent Criminal Apprehension Program shall be entered as soon as possible.

e. Nothing is this section shall be construed to preclude a law enforcement agency from obtaining any of the materials identified in this section before the 30th day following the filing of the missing person report.

5. Upon the initial receipt of a missing person report, a law enforcement agency shall seek to determine whether the person reported missing is high risk.

a. A high-risk missing person is an individual whose whereabouts are not currently known and the circumstances indicate that the individual may be at risk of injury or death. The circumstances that indicate that an individual is high-risk missing person shall include, but not be limited to:

(1) the person is missing as a result of a stranger abduction;

(2) the person is missing under suspicious circumstances;

(3) the person is missing under unknown circumstances;

(4) the person is missing under known dangerous circumstances;

(5) the person is missing more than 30 days;

(6) the person has already been designated as a high-risk missing person by another law enforcement agency;

(7) there is evidence that the person is at risk because:

(a) the person missing is in need of medical attention, or prescription medication;

(b) the person missing does not have a pattern of running away or disappearing;

(c) the person missing may have been abducted by a noncustodial parent;

(d) the person missing is mentally impaired;

(e) the person missing is a person under the age of 21 years; or

(f) the person missing has been the subject of past threats or acts of violence.

(8) any other factor that may, in the judgment of the chief of the law enforcement agency receiving the missing person report, determine that the missing person may be at risk.

b. A finding that a person reported missing is not high risk shall not preclude a later determination, based on further investigation or the discovery of additional information, that the missing person is high risk.

6. a. When a law enforcement agency determines that a missing person is a high-risk missing person it shall notify the State Police Missing Persons Unit. It shall immediately provide the State Police Missing Persons Unit with the information that is most likely to aid in the location and safe return of the high-risk missing person. As soon as practicable, the law enforcement agency shall provide all other information obtained relating to the missing person case to the State Police Missing Persons Unit.

b. The State Police Missing Persons Unit shall promptly notify all law enforcement agencies within the State and, if deemed appropriate, law enforcement agencies in adjacent states or jurisdictions of the information that may aid in the prompt location and safe return of the high-risk missing person;

c. Local law enforcement agencies that receive notification from the State Police Missing Unit pursuant to subsection b. of this section shall forward that information immediately to its officers and members.

d. The State Police Missing Persons Unit shall, as appropriate, enter all collected information relating to the missing person case to applicable Federal databases. The information shall be provided in accordance with applicable guidelines relating to the databases, as follows:

(1) a missing person report, and relevant information, in a high risk missing person case shall be entered in the National Crime Information Center database immediately, but in no case no more than 2 hours of the determination that the missing person is a high risk missing person.

(2) a missing person report, and relevant information, in a case not involving a high risk missing person shall be entered within 24 hours of the initial filing of the missing person report.

(3) all DNA profiles shall be uploaded into the missing persons databases of the New Jersey Forensic DNA Laboratory and all appropriate and suitable federal database systems.

(4) information relevant to the Federal Bureau of Investigation's Violent Criminal Apprehension Program shall be entered as soon as practicable.

(5) all due care shall be given to insure that the data, particularly medical and dental records, entered in State and federal database systems is accurate and, to the greatest extent possible, complete.

(6) the State Police shall, when deemed appropriate and likely to facilitate a resolution to a particular missing person report, activate the Amber Alert program for the State.

7. a. The Attorney General shall provide information to local law enforcement agencies about best practices and protocols for handling death scene investigations;

b. The Attorney General shall identify any publications or training opportunities that may be available to local law enforcement officers concerning the handling of death scene investigations.

8. a. After performing any death scene investigation, as deemed appropriate under the circumstances, the official with custody of the human remains shall ensure that the

human remains are delivered to the appropriate county medical examiner.

b. Any county medical examiner with custody of human remains that are not identified within 24 hours of discovery shall promptly notify the State Police of the location of those remains.

c. If the county medical examiner with custody of remains cannot determine whether or not the remains found are human, the medical examiner shall so notify the State Police.

9. a. If the official with custody of the human remains is not a medical examiner, the official shall promptly transfer the unidentified remains to the appropriate county medical examiner.

b. The county medical examiner shall make reasonable attempts to promptly identify human remains. These actions may include but are not limited to obtaining:

(1) photographs of the human remains;

(2) dental or skeletal X-rays;

(3) photographs of items found with the human remains;

(4) fingerprints from the remains, if possible;

(5) samples of tissue suitable for DNA typing, if possible;

(6) samples of whole bone and/or hair suitable for DNA typing;

(7) any other information that may support identification efforts.

c. No medical examiner or any other person shall, dispose of, or engage in actions that will materially affect the unidentified human remains before the county medical examiner obtains:

(1) samples suitable for DNA identification archiving;

(2) photographs of the unidentified human remains; and

(3) all other appropriate steps for identification have been exhausted.

d. Unidentified human remains shall not be cremated.

e. The county medical examiner shall make reasonable efforts to obtain prompt DNA analysis of biological samples, if the human remains have not been identified by other means within 30 days.

f. The medical examiner shall seek support from appropriate State and federal agencies to assist in the identification of unidentified human remains. Such assistance may include, but not be limited to, available mitochondrial or nuclear DNA testing, federal grants for DNA testing, or federal grants for crime laboratory or medical examiner office improvement.

g. The county medical examiner shall promptly enter information in federal and State databases that can aid in the identification of a missing person. Information shall be entered into federal databases as follows:

(1) information for the National Crime Information Center within 24 hours;

(2) DNA profiles and information 1 shall be entered into the National DNA Index System (NDIS) within five business days after the completion of the DNA analysis and procedures necessary for the entry of the DNA profile; and

(3) information sought by the Violent Criminal Apprehension Program database as soon as practicable.

h. Nothing in this act shall be construed to preclude any medical examiner office, the State Police or any local law enforcement agency from other actions to facilitate the identification of unidentified human remains including efforts to publicize information, descriptions or photographs that may aid in the identification of the unidentified remains, including allowing family members to identify a missing person; provided that in taking these actions, all due consideration is given to protect the dignity and well-being of the of the missing person and the family of the missing person.

i. Agencies handling the remains of a missing person who is deceased shall notify the law enforcement agency handling the missing person's case. Documented efforts must be made to locate family members of the deceased person to inform them of the death and location of the remains of their family member.

10. The Attorney General, pursuant to the provisions of the 'Administrative Procedure Act,' P.L.1968, c.410 (C.52:14B-1 et seq.), shall promulgate rules and regulations to effectuate the purposes of this act.

11. This act shall take effect on the first day of the seventh month following enactment, but the Attorney General may take such anticipatory administrative action in advance as shall be necessary for the implementation of this act.

STATEMENT
This bill, to be known as 'Patricia's Law,' is model missing persons legislation proposed by the National Criminal

Justice Reference Service, a federally funded resource center that supports research, policy and program development in the criminal justice area.

The purpose of this model legislation is to improve the ability of law enforcement to locate and return missing persons, to improve the identification of human remains and to improve timely information and notification to the family members of missing persons.

The bill outlines the best practices and protocols law enforcement should adopt and utilize in missing person cases, identifying human remains and in providing timely information to the families of missing persons to keep them fully apprised and aware of the actions being taken and the progress made in their investigation.

TIMELINE

THE FIRST NINE MONTHS

2007

3 May – Madeleine McCann is reported missing by her parents Kate and Gerry McCann while the family is holidaying in Praia da Luz in southern Portugal.

4 May – Police dogs are brought in to pick up the scent of the missing child while volunteer teams comb the village and beach for clues.

5 May – Detectives consider abduction and say they have a sketch of a potential suspect.

7 May – Kate McCann appears on television to make an emotional plea to her daughter's abductor.

10 May – Police wind down the ground search for Madeleine. 350 potential leads have produced no breakthrough for investigators.

12 May – Madeleine's fourth birthday. Celebrities including Sir

Richard Branson, author JK Rowling and Sir Philip Green of Topshop donate towards a £2.5 million reward offered for information leading to Madeleine's safe return. Criticism is aimed at the public campaign and resources by local parents whose children have previously disappeared in Portugal.

14 May – Police search the home of Anglo-Portuguese resident Robert Murat. Following interrogation, Murat is given *arguido* status in the case, making him the first official suspect for the abduction.

16 May – Detectives search the home of Russian IT expert Sergei Malinka, suspected of being an associate of Murat.

17 May – The McCanns' helpers launch a special Find Madeleine website, raising £1 million to help in the search.

23 May – The McCanns travel to the Marian site at Fatima to pray for their daughter's safe return.

25 May – Police release the description of a man seen carrying a child near the McCanns' apartment on the night of Madeleine's abduction. The sketch has no facial features and is ridiculed by the UK press.

30 May – The McCanns begin their campaign to raise awareness of Madeleine with a visit to Pope Benedict XVI in Rome. This is followed by meetings with officials and politicians in Germany, Morocco, Holland, Spain and the USA.

6 June – In an interview in Berlin, the shocked couple first hear of the suspicions of their involvement in their daughter's disappearance from a reporter.

13 June – Police in Praia da Luz search an area of deserted scrubland near the village following an anonymous tip-off published in a Dutch newspaper.

21 June – Sightings of children resembling Madeleine are reported in Malta, Morocco, Spain, France, Switzerland, Belgium, Argentina and Guatemala.

11 July – Robert Murat is recalled to Portimão police station for further questioning. Rachael Oldfield, Fiona Payne and Russell O'Brien claim they saw a man matching his description near the McCanns' apartment on 3 May.

23 July – Gerry McCann flies to the US to meet Attorney General Alberto Gonzales to discuss child abduction in the country. His controlled demeanour in the world spotlight receives criticism in the UK and Portuguese press.

3 Aug – Belgian police release a sketch of a couple seen with a girl resembling Madeleine in Tongeren. In Praia da Luz, police dig up the garden of the villa that Robert Murat shares with his mother, Jennifer.

7 Aug – Traces of blood are found in Madeleine's bedroom by British sniffer dogs specially flown in from the UK.

7 Aug – Accusations that they accidentally killed Madeleine and hid her body are levelled at the McCanns in the Portuguese press.

15 Aug – Portuguese investigators acknowledge that Madeleine may be dead after a corpse dog is reported to have detected the trace smell of a cadaver inside apartment 5A.

21 Aug – Investigators present their theory that Madeleine died in the apartment by accident.

29 Aug – Gerry McCann walks out of a Spanish TV interview in response to probing questions about his and his wife's possible involvement in their daughter's death.

1 Sept – The investigation spotlight shifts to the McCanns as police report 'significant' results from the forensic tests carried out in Birmingham.

6 Sept – Kate McCann is formally questioned by police in Portimão.

7 Sept – Madeleine's parents are declared official suspects in the investigation.

9 Sept – The McCanns fly home to Rothley with twins Sean and Amelie.

11 Sept – Police announce that DNA samples offering a '100 %' match to Madeleine have been found in the McCanns' hire car and holiday apartment. A file is passed to the Public Prosecutor.

12 Sept – The Portuguese Public Prosecutor requests UK police seize Kate McCann's diary and Madeleine's soft toy, Cuddle Cat.

13 Sept – A report in a French newspaper that Madeleine died from an overdose of sleeping tablets is denied by British forensic experts.

16 Sept – Five Portuguese detectives, including DCI Gonçalo Amaral, are charged with misconduct resulting from interrogations of Leonor Cipriano in 2004.

17 Sept – American lawyers who have successfully proved in a recent case the inaccuracy of corpse dogs in scenting cadavers are contacted by the McCanns' lawyers.

18 Sept – Justine McGuinness resigns as the McCanns' family spokesman to be replaced by ex-Foreign Office Director of Media Liaison Clarence Mitchell. Gordon Brown is rumoured to be behind the changeover.

19 Sept – The Portuguese Public Prosecutor for the Algarve rules there is insufficient evidence to reinterrogate the McCanns.

25 Sept – A woman is photographed in Morocco carrying a child who resembles Madeleine McCann. The child is later identified as five-year-old Bushra Binhisa.

3 Oct – Judicial Police Inspector Gonçalo Amaral is removed from the inquiry after his public criticism of the British police. In the same month, the McCann camp hires Spanish detective agency Método 3 on a six-month contract costing £30,000.

3 Nov – A special appeal for help in finding Madeleine is broadcast by Kate McCann. A week later, a meeting takes place between the McCanns and their holiday companions at a Leicester hotel.

25 Dec – Find Madeleine Fund launches a special Christmas Appeal.

2008

13 Jan – In a book by Correio da Manhã editor-in-chief Manuel Catarino, top Portuguese forensic specialist Jose Manuel Anes blames the McCanns for 'misdirecting' the police by insisting their daughter had been abducted.

15 Jan – An identikit is published of a gaunt stranger seen by holidaymaker Gail Cooper, apparently stalking children in the week before Madeleine McCann's disappearance. Portimão says the man was traced and eliminated early in the inquiry.

20 Jan – News is released that Kate and Gerry McCann are

in talks regarding a £1 million book deal and film offers for their story. The report is quickly denied.

3 Feb – In an interview on Portuguese radio, the National Director of Portugal's Judicial Police, Alípio Ribeiro, says it is possible that detectives were 'too hasty' in naming Gerry and Kate McCann as suspects in the disappearance of their daughter.

5 Feb – The Office of the Portuguese Attorney General says there are no plans to remove the McCanns from the list of official suspects. Along with Robert Murat, they may remain *arguidos* until the case is closed, which may take years...